JEFFERSON COUNTY, GEORGIA INFERIOR COURT MINUTES

July 1797 - April 1800

By

Michael A. Ports

CLEARFIELD

Printed for Clearfield Company by
Genealogical Publishing Company
Baltimore, Maryland
2015

ISBN 978-0-8063-5767-6

Introduction

The Georgia General Assembly created Jefferson County February 20, 1796, from parts of Burke and Warren Counties, making Louisville the seat of its new government. The Inferior Court, made up of five justices of the peace for the county, tried any civil case except those involving title to land. The Inferior Court had jurisdiction over county business matters, such as care for the poor, building and maintaining the courthouse and jails, building and maintaining roads and bridges, issuing licenses to sell liquor, nominating justices of the peace, performing naturalizations, appointing guardians, authorized indentures, and maintaining a register of wills. The Clerk of the Inferior Court kept minutes of its various proceedings.

The first volume of Inferior Court Minutes begins July 11, 1797 and continues through April 13, 1800. The following transcription comes from the microfilm of the original record book made in 1958 at Louisville, by the Genealogical Society of Salt Lake City, Utah and available at the Georgia Department of Archives and History in Morrow, Georgia and the Family History Library. The volume includes an index of names and subjects that is not transcribed here. Instead, a new full name index follows the transcription. The numbers between brackets [ ] are the original page numbers. Following the court minutes, on the last page of the original volume, the clerk recorded a Docket of Executions Returnable to the December Term 1797.

Deputy Clerk John L. Dixon kept the minutes from the beginning until December 7, 1797, when Clerk James Bozeman began keeping the minutes. For the most part, the handwriting of the two men is legible, making the transcription straightforward and not too difficult. The occasional ink smear or other imperfection is noted in brackets, for eample [illegible]. Sometimes, both men formed the small letters "a" and "o" in a very similar manner, making abbreviations such as Jas. and Jos. impossible to distinguish. Their formation of the letters "n" and "r" at the end of surnames make it difficult to distinguish the name Barrier from Barrien, for example. Also, the two clerks formed the capital letters "I" and "J" indentically. Determining which letter usually is straightforward when the first letter of a name, but entirely a guess when an initial. The transcription follows Sperry's recommended guidelines for reading early script.[1] The transcription does not correct any grammar or spelling, no matter how obvious the errors, but does add a few commas for clarity. Finally, the clerks entered a vertical squiggly line to delineate lawsuit citations and other headings, duplicated by the symbol } in the transcription.

The court minutes contain numerous original signatures. Upon each day's adjournment, the clerk and each of the attending justices signed their names attesting to the accuracy of the minutes. Jury foremen signed their verdicts. Losing defendants and their securities signed the judgments against them. On February 16, 1799, the Georgia Legislature passed an act compelling all county civil and military officers to take and subscribe to an oath of allegiance to

---

[1] Sperry, Kip, *Reading Early American Handwriting*. Genealogical Publishing Company, Inc., Baltimore, Maryland, Sixth Printing, 2008.

the state constitution. On April 1, 1799, the clerk recorded the oath and, after taking the oath each of the officers signed and dated the minutes, some as late as February 1803.

The book is dedicated to the memory of Hardy and Barbara Harrell, who were early settlers of that part of Warren County that became Jefferson Couty in 1796, two of the author's numerous Georgia ancestors. Many thanks are offered to Joe Garonzik, of the Genealogical Publishing Company, for his sound advice and counsel. Special thanks are offered to Marcia Tremonti for her patience and encouragement during this challenging endeavor.

Georgia, Jefferson County } At an Inferior Court held in and for the County aforesaid on the 11th day of July 1796, present their honors, John Shellman, Solomon Woods, Douglas Hancock, Michael Shellman, Esquires. [1]

William Paulett came into Court and qualified as deputy Sheriff.

The following persons were appointed Constables and qualified according to Law: Viz. James Harvie for Capt. Tandy Key's Dist., Britain McCullers for Becoms District, Pearson Young for Capt. Terry's Distr., John Powell for Capt. Rhode's district, Samuel McNeely for Capt. Alexander's Dist., Ephraim Chance for Capt. Raiford's District, John Mackey for Louisville District.

The Court adjourned till tomorrow morning nine o'clock. [2]

John Shellman, S. Woods, Douglass Hancock. Test. J. L. Dixon, for Clk. of Inf. Court.

Tuesday morning, 9 o'clock, July 12th 1796. The Court met according to adjournment, present their honors, John Shellman, Douglass Hancock, Michl Shellman, Solomon Wood, Esquires.

Ordered that Thomas Whitehead, William Hardwick, and John Reis be and they are appointed Commissioners to view and report the propriety and necessity of opening a road from Rocky Comfort where Gates bridge formerly stood to cross Duhart's Creek at the Chickasaw ford

from thence the most direct way to Augusta, as far as the County Line. [3]

Ordered that Isaac Coleman, Charles Harvey, and Samuel Andrews be continued as Commissioners for opening a road leading from Louisville to Georgetown, agreeably to an order of Warren Court, and that they or a majority of them complete the same or make such alteration as they may deem proper and they are hereby directed to extend the same to Louisville.

Ordered that Zachariah Fenn, Peter Kolb, and Charles Coats be and are hereby appointed Commissioners to view and report the propriety and necessity of opening a road from Fenn's bridge on Ogechee to the town of Louisville.

Ordered that John Parsons, William Neel, and Stephen Powell be and are hereby appointed Commissioners to view and report the propriety and necessity of opening a road from Louisville to Powell's Bridge on Ogechee, from thence to Wood's Bridge on Williamson's

Swamp, and from thence toward Montgomery Court House, till it intersects the [4]
County Line.

Ordered that Mathew Carswell and William Clements be and are hereby appointed Commissioners, immediately to proceed, to put, and keep in good repair, the road leading from Louisville to Waynesborough, as far as the County line extends.

Ordered that Samuel Gordon be and he is hereby appointed Commissioner for keeping in repair the road leading from Walker's Bridge to Louisville from the County line to where it intersects the Waynesborough road.

Ordered that David Jameson, esqr. And William Brackett be are are hereby appointed Commissioners to keep in good repair the road leading from Louisville to Savannah till it intersects the County line.

Ordered that John Barrier, Jesse Womack, and Richd D. Gray be and are hereby appointed Commissioners in lieu of John Parsons, Blassingham

Harvey, Sr., and Zachariah Gray (who were appointed by the hon^{l} the Inferior [5]
Court of Burke County) to open a road from Louisville leading the most direct and convenient way, towards the town of Washington, Wilkes County, the said Commissioners are hereby directed to open and keep in good repair the said road till it intersects the County line.

Ordered that Robert Reed, Joseph Jackson, and Robert Maxwell be continued to act as Commissioners for opening and keeping in good repair a road leading from Vivian's Bridge on Williamson's Swamp to cross the Ogechee river at Shellman's Bridge and so on to Louisville and that they be authorized to call on one fourth of the citizens of Louisville to work on the said road to Ogechee river.

Ordered that Pearson Young, David Terry, and Benjamin Darsey be and they are hereby appointed Commissioners to view and report the propriety and necessity of opening a road from Danelly's Bridge on Brier Creek to Thomas Whitehead's.

Ordered that Richard Gray, esq. be allowed the sum of Two hundred and forty [6]
eight dollars for running marking out the County lines of Jefferson and for expenses incurred therein, that he shall receive one hundred and fifty dollars thereof, so soon as it may come into the hands of the Clerk, who is hereby directed to pay the same out of the first monies that may come into his hands from the Collector of said County.

Ordered that the one fourth and one sixth parts of the of the general tax for the last and present years be levied as a County tax agreeably to Law, and the Collector of the County of Jefferson is hereby authorized to collect the same after having given bond and security in double the amount thereof to one or more of the Justices of the Inferior Court for the due performance of the duties required of him by Law.

Ordered that William McGehee, John Cobbs, and Michael Shellman, esquires, be and [7]
are hereby appointed Commissioners to put and keep in good repair the Bridge and causeway across Rocky Comfort by the place known as Lawson's Old Bridge, and they are hereby authorized to contract with some person for the same, that one hundred dollars be paid to the said Commissioners in part, out of the monies arising from the County tax of the last and present years, and the remainder if any to be applied out of some future appropriation.

Ordered that John Hartsfield be and he is hereby appointed Constable for Captain Gray's District.

Ordered that William Hardwick, William Vining, and Isaac Coleman be and are hereby appointed Commissioners to contract with some person to build a Bridge to cross Rocky Comfort at or near the place

where Gates' Bridge formerly stood, that the Commissioners are hereby directed [8]
and required to take bond of the undertakers with sufficient security to keep the same in good repair for the term of five years, and that the price thereof shall not exceed the sum of one hundred dollars, and that fifty dollars be paid in part thereof out of the last and present years' County tax, and the balance out of the County tax of the succeeding year.

Ordered the Clerk of this Court forward the different Commissioners of roads and Bridges herein appointed with a Copy of the orders to that effect.

Ordered that the Clerk contract with some person to make a seal with the following inscription (to wit) inf. Court Jefferson fiat Justicia, with the Sword of Justice in the centre.

The Court adjourned till Court in course. John Shellman, Douglass Hancock [9]
M. Shelman. Test. J. L. Dixon for Clk. Of Inf. Court

October 6, 1796. A list of Jurors drawn for December Term 1796. Present their Honors John Shelman, Michael Shellman.

1. John Hale
2. Jno. Smith
3. Jas. Boyd
4. Jno. Nelson
5. Jno. Dupree
6. Jesse Horn

12. Jacob Colson
13. Thos Sandford
14. Jno. Bigham
15. Saml Cockrill
16. Absalom Prior
17. Bennett Abbott

7. Saml Briggs
8. Derrix Wothen
9. Jno. Flennnury
10. Joseph Lockheart
11. Arch^{d} Letler

18. Dav^{d} Shores
19. Jas. Anderson
20. Jos. Price
21. Robt Wood
22. Nathan Ross

23. Philip Calhoun
24. Jesse Hatcher
25. Abram Lefever
26. Jordan Hargrove
27. Saml Flemming
28. Jos. Chastain
29. Richd Spiers
30. John Marchant
31. John Neely
32. Jno. Harrington
33. Jno. Vining
34. Jno. Armstrong
35. W. Coats
36. Jonas Mays
37. James Trowell
38. Enoch Trowell
39. Wm Hart
40. John Whigham
41. Geo. Prince
42. Richd Fleeting
43. Danl McNeely
44. Tho. Fulton
45. Absalom Coursey

46. Tho. Lark [10]
47. Tho. Gay
48. Jno. Thompson
49. Tho. Wasden, Jr.
50. Robt Prior
51. Saml McBrade
52. Strocow Crawford
53. Henry Jordon
54. Robert Stevenson
55. Reuben Wasden
56. Pat McCulloch
57. James Smith
58. Robert McEl John
59. Gilbert McNair
60. Henry Wolden
61. Henry Wall
62. Wm Coleman
63. Robt Pateman
64. Jas. Bozeman
65. Wm Dawkins, Jr.
66. Thomas Rogers
67. Jno. Newman
68. Jas. Manson
69. Will: Hadden, Jr.
70. Meshack Mathews
71. Wm Mathews
72. Peter Mathews

At an Inferior Court held in and for the County of Jefferson of the 12th day of December [12]
1796. Present their honors. Douglass Hancock, Solomon Wood, John Clements, Esquires.

Jurors called & sworn.

1. Joseph Prior
2. Thomas Wasden

Jno. M. Whitney

3. John Hale
4. Robt. McEl John
5. Jos. Chastain
6. Saml McBride
7. Jesse Hatcher
8. Jno. Vining
9. Patrick McCulloch
10. Saml Briggs
11. James Boyd
12. Tho. Fulton

vs
G. R. Ragan
Judgement by default

Robert Walker
vs
P. Crookshanks
Judgement by default

E. Brenan } [13]
vs } Note
Peter Chastain }

Dismissed at the Plaintiffs Costs

The Court adjourned till tomorrow ten o'clock. Attest J. L. Dixon, Asst. Clk.

Tuesday, December 13, 1796. The Court met agreeably to adjournment. Present Their Honors Solomon Woods, John Clements, M. Shelman, Esqrs.

On the Petition of a number of the Inhabitants of Capt. Tarver's District to have George Ingram appointed Constable. Thereupon ordered that said Ingram be and is hereby appointed, came into Court and was qualified accordingly.

D. McDuff } Detinue [14]
vs } Continued by consent
M. Shellman }

Same } Detinue
vs } Continued by consent
Fran^{s} Coleman }

Settled at Plfts cost, except the monies, in which is paid by the defendant.

On the Complaint of Page Tally, an apprentice to T. Collins by Peter Williamson his attorney, setting forth that he is not treated by said Collins as an apprentice right to be treated by a master, and suffers, evidence being introduced to this court to that effect, thereupon ordered, that he the said Page Tally be released from his Indenture and his recognizance wherein he was bound to appear at this Court. & the Indenture be made a record of that Court.

Court Adjourned till tomorrow, ten o'clock. Attest. J. L. Dixon

Wednesday, August 3rd 1796 [15]

The Court met agreeably to adjournment.

Present their Honors. Douglass Hancock, M. Shelman, Jno. Clements, Esqs.

Danl McNeely }
vs } Attachment
Robt Hopper } Judgement by default.

Robt Walker }
vs } Attachment
Pat. Crookshanks }

Jurors sworn in this case.

1. Frank Coleman, Sr.
2. John Paulet
3. F. Coleman, Jr.
4. Jno. Downer
5. C. Hardwick
6. Page Tally
7. Thos. Fulton
8. P. McCulloch
9. Robt Maxwell
10. Wm Fokes
11. Jesse Hatcher
12. Joseph Chairs

Daniel Sturgis, Esq., who was summoned as a Garnishee in this case declares on oath that [16]
he has in his possession twenty nine plats of land lying in Franklin County, each platt containing one thousand acres.

We the jury find for the Plaintiff Robert Walker two hundred forty nine pounds, eight & nine pence, half penny in Dollars at four & eight pence equal to one thousand and sixty new dollars & two cents.

Wm Hardwick, foreman

Danl McNeely }
vs } Attachment
Robt Hopper }

Same Jury as above.

We the Jury find for the Plaintiff Daniel McNeely, three hundred dollars.

Wm Hardwick, foreman

Danl McDuff } [17]
vs } Detinue
Fran^{s} Coleman }

On motion of Peter Williams, atty for Champness Terry, it is ordered that the said Terry be & he is hereby made a Defendant in the case of Danl McDuff against Francis Coleman and that he the said Terry may be intitled to all the privileges as tho he had been sued originally & jointly with the said Francis Coleman.

Robt Walker }
vs } Attachment
Pat. Crookshanks }

Dan Glinger, Esq., who was summoned as a Garnishee in the above case, declares on oath that he has in his possession twenty nine plats for land lying in Franklin County, each plat containing one thousand acres.

John M. Whitney } [18]
vs } Attachment
George N. Ragan }

Daniel Sturgis, Esq., a Garnishee in this case, states upon oath that he has in his possession twelve plats of land for one thousand acres each, in the name of George N. Ragan lying in the county of McIntosh on the Alatamaka river.

On the application of William Hardwick, Esq., Receiver of the Tax, returns for the [19]
county of Jefferson to be allowed two and one half ¢ Cash on all Taxes arising from the property returned, and it appearing to the Court that the Law authorizes him to receive the same. Therefore, Ordered, that the Clerk do give him a Certificate to that effect.

The Court adjourned till Wednesday, the 28th of the Month. Douglass Hancock, John Clements, M. Shelman. Attest. J. Dixon, dep. Clk.

Wednesday, 28th December 1796 [20]
The Honorable the Inferior Court met agreeably to adjournment. Present their Honors, Douglass Hancock, Michael Shelman, John Clements, Esquires.

Ordered that John Berrier, Esq. immediately call one fourth of the hands belonging to Louisville together and proceed to open the Road in a direct line to Boyd's and from thence repair the old road to Clayton's Mill. And that Zachariah Gray be appointed in lieu of Richard Gray, to keep in repair the road leading from Clayton's Mill to Neely's branch and that Thomas Elliott be appointed in lieu of Jesse Wamack to open and keep in good repair the road leading from Neely's branch to the ford on Duhart's Creek at Nathaniel Samples, and that John Moulard be & he is hereby appointed in addition to the above

Commissioners to open and keep in good repair the road leading from Nathaniel [21]
Samples the most direct way to the town of Washington as far the County line agreeably to a former Order of the Court.

Ordered that John L. Dixon, James Rogers & William Hardwick be and they are hereby appointed Commissioners to open & keep in good repair the old road leading from Boyd's to Loury & James Rogers as far as the County line.

Ordered that the road from Louisville to Fenns Bridge run as follows, from Louisville to Cobbs pond from thence to the old School house on Camp branch from thence to the said Bridge and that Shadrach Vining, Peter Kobb, and Morris Murphy be and they are hereby appointed Commissioners to open & keep in good repair the said Road.

Ordered that the road from Louisville to the Montgomery County line be established as follows to wit, from Louisville to Powells Bridge, from thence to Woods Bridge on Williamsons Swamp, and so on in a direct

way to the County line – and that Thompson Lawson, William Neel & Stephen Powell [22]
be and are hereby appointed Commissioners ~~to act with in lieu of John Parsons~~ to open and keep in good repair the same, and that all the hands below Louisville in the fork of Big Creek South side of the Savannah road, be subject to work on the said Road.

Ordered, that Bird Tarver & Moses Horn, be and they are hereby appointed Commissioners to keep in good repair the road leading from Big Creek to Col^{o} John Jones Mill as far as the County line.

Ordered that, Samuel Andrews, John Reis, and Stephen Morgan be and they are hereby appointed Commissioners to run and report the necessity of a Road from Fenns Bridge to Thomas Whiteheads to cross convenient & direct way.

Ordered that John Marshall, Hugh Alexander & Alexander Carswell, be and they are [23]
hereby appointed Commissioners to open and keep in good repair the Road leading from Louisville to Jacksonboro and that they immediately proceed to act accordingly.

Ordered that Sanders Bush, John Vining, and John Peel be and they are hereby appointed Commissioners to open & keep in good repair the old Road leading from Gateses Bridge on Rocky Comfort to Thomas Whiteheads.

The following persons were drawn to serve as Jurors at July Term 1797.

1. Wm Boon
2. Nat Sample, Ju^{n}
3. Wm Harris

11. Tho. Tensley
12. Adam Calhoun
13. Jno Kenneday, Junr

4. Tho. Little, Jun.
5. Wm Scott
6. Wm Darsey
7. Wm Young, Senr
8. Ja^{s} Blair
9. Jesse Hollandsworth
10. Danl McNeal

14. Robert Hale
15. Jno Manson
16. Wm Fountain, Sen.
17. Henry Cox
18. M. Forsyth
19. A. Berryhill
20. Dav^{d} Terry

21. Jno Willson
22. Tho. Hamilton
23. Howell Hargrove
24. Thos Neely
25. Elijah Kersey
26. Sam Gordch
27. Richd Womack
28. Stephen Morgan

29. Jno Brook., Jr [24]
30. Ja^{s} Weeks
31. Dav^{d} McGowan
32. Isaac Rawls
33. John Mocke
34. Jno Peterson
35. Arch Boyd
36. James Hart

Court adjourned till Court in Course. Douglas Hancock, M. Shelman, J. Clements
Teste. J. L. Dixon, Dep. Clk.

At an Inferior Court began and held in and for the County of Jefferson at the House of Joseph Chairs, on Tuesday 11 July 1797. [25]

Present. Their honors John Shellman, John Clements, Douglas Hancock, M. Shelman

Daniel McNeely }
vs } Attachment
Robert Hopper }

Judgment at December Term 1796 for three hundred Dollars

On motion of Plaintiffs Counsel and it appearing that the above Attachment has been levied, on two hundred acres of land.

It is ordered that the Sheriff proceed to sell the same towards the satisfaction of said Judgment in terms of the Judiciary act, in such cases made and provided.

Jurors called & sworn

1. Wm Boon
2. Wm Harris
3. Tho. Little
4. John Blair

7. Wm Fontain
8. Jno Mocke
9. Jno Wilson
10. Tho. Neely

5. John Kenneday, Jr
6. John Manson
11. Sam[l] Gordon
12. Rich[d] Womack

Rob[t] Walker }
vs } Attachment
P. Crookshanks } [26]

Judgment at December Term 1796 for one thousand & sixty nine dollars & two Cents.

On motion of Plaintiffs Counsel and it appearing that the above Attachment has been levied, on twenty nine thousand acres of land in the County of Franklin.

It is ordered that the Sheriff proceed to sell the same towards the satisfaction of said Judgment in terms of the Judiciary act, in such cases made and provided.

On the application of Thomas Douglas.

It is ordered, that in consequence of his extreme indigence, that he be, and he is hereby declared free from Poll Tax.

On the application of James Cox.

It is ordered, that in consequence of his extreme indigence, that he be, and he is hereby declared free from Poll Tax.

The Court adjourned till tomorrow 9 o'clock. [27]

Wednesday 12 July 1797

The Court met agreeably to adjournment. present Their Honors John Shellman, Douglas Hancock, John Clements, Michael Shelman, Solomon Wood, Justices of Inf. Court.

William Smith } Slander
vs } Settled at Plffs Costs
John Neeland }

Daniel McElduff }
vs } Detinue
Michael Shelman } Dismissed, at the Plaintiffs Cost

Daniel McElduff } Witnesses Sworn [28]
vs } Detinue W[m] Coleman
Francis Coleman } John Lewis

Jurors Sworn

1. William Boon	7. William Fountain
2. William Harris	8. John Mocke
3. Thomas Little	9. John Wilson
4. John Blair	10. Thomas Neely
5. John Kenneday, Jr.	11. Sam[l] Gordon
6. John Manson	12. Rich[d] Womack

We of the Jury find for the Defendant with cost of suit. Samuel Gordon, foreman.

John Towns }
vs } Special Case
Dan[l] McElduff } Continued

Rob[t] Spears, for }
the use of R. Quarles } Debt
vs }
S. Hammond } Discontinued at the Plaintiffs cost.

Champness Terry } [29]
vs } Trover
Francis Coleman }

Zachariah Fenn, John Taylor & Richard Gray came into Court and entered themselves Special bail for the defendant in the above cause, to pay the condemnation money thereof in case he shall be cast therein or surrender the defendant into Court in discharge thereof.

Champness Terry }
vs } Trover
Francis Coleman }

Same Jury as in McElduff & Coleman. Witnesses sworn. M. Shelman

We of the Jury find no cause of action against Francis Coleman, the Defendant.
Sam[l] Gordon, foreman

Isaac Chance } [30]
vs } Debt
John Styron & }
Mat Dorton }

James Harvey & Thomas Harvey came into Court and entered special bail for the Defendants, in the above cause to pay the eventual condemnation money shou'd they be cast, or render them upto the Court in discharge thereof.

Ordered that Abram Peerce be and is hereby appointed Constable in Captain Rhode's District, and that Samuel Samford and Ephraim Chance be and they are hereby appointed Constables in Captain Raiford's District, they gave bond and qualified agreeable to Law.

Cheslie Bostick, Jr. }
vs } Carr.
Henry Shaffer }

John Lewis & Joseph Rees came into Court, and entered special bail in the above case, to pay the eventual condemnation money shou'd the defendant be cast or render the body of the defendant in discharge thereof.

The Court adjourned till tomorrow 9 o'clock. [31]
Test. J. L. Dixon Dep. Clk.

Wednesday 13th July 1797. The Court met agreeably to adjournment.

Present. Their Honors Michael Shellman, Solomon Wood, John Clements, Douglas Hancock

1. William Boon
2. William Harris
3. Thomas Little
4. John Brook
5. John Kenneday
6. John Manson
7. William Fountain
8. John Mocke
9. John Wilson
10. Thomas Neely
11. Saml Gordon
12. Richd Womack

Thomas Collings }
vs } Case
Joseph G. Posner } Discontinued at the Plffs cost.

Jane McBride } [32]
vs } Debt
Danl McNeely } Settled at Defendants cost

John Bostick & Co. }
vs } Case
Zachariah Gray }

John Cobbs came into Court and entered Special bail in the above case to pay the eventual condemnation money shou'd the defend[t] be cast or render the body of the Defendant in discharge thereof.

Tubman, Patey & Tubman }
vs } Case
Zachariah Gray }

John Cobbs came into Court and entered Special bail in the above case to pay the eventual condemnation money shou'd the defendant be cast or render the body of the Defendant in discharge thereof.

Woods assignee of } [33]
O'Daniel } Covenant
vs }
F. Clemm } Continued

William Jenkins }
vs } Trover
Michael Shelman } Continued

Levin Collins }
vs } Case
Zachariah Gray } Witness Major Collins, Thomas Morely

The same jury as before. We find for the plaintiff Sixty four dollars with Interest & cost of suit.
Samuel Gordon, foreman

John M. Whitney }
vs } Attachment
Geo. N. Ragan } Continued by consent

Bailey Harrell }
vs } Case
Harvey & Key }

We of the Jury find for Bailey Harrell the plaintiff thirty two dollars with lawful interest from the date due with cost of suit. Sam[l] Gordon, foreman

Jeremiah Oats } Witness sworn Ja[s] Harvey [34]
vs }
Jesse Paulett } Case

Same jury as before. We of the Jury find for Jeremiah Oats the plaintiff thirty two dollars with lawful interest from the date due with cost of suit. Sam[l] Gordon, foreman

Jane McBride }
vs } Debt
Dan[l] McNeely } Continued

John Shelman }
vs } Attachment
John Anderson }

The defendant in the above case being called and not answering. Judgment went against him by Default.

Harrell }
vs }
Harvey & Key }

The defendant came into Court with John Cobbs their security who acknowledged himself bound with the defendants for the day of execution in terms of the Act.

John Shelman } [35]
vs } Attachment
John Anderson }

Same jury as before. We find for the plaintiff four hundred and Twenty eight dollars fifty three Cents principal & sixty dollars interest with cost of suit. Sam[l] Gordon, foreman

On motion of Mr. Corner, attorney for John Shelman, and it appearing that the above attachment has been levied on one hundred acres of land in Jefferson County. It is ordered that the Sheriff proceed to sell the same towards the satisfaction of the Judgment in terms of the Judiciary Act in such cases made and provided.

Levin Collins }
vs } Case
Zach. Gray }

The defendant came into Court with John Cobbs his Security who acknowledged himself bound with the said Z. Gray for the stay of execution in Terms of the Act.

Patrick Carr } [36]
vs } Settled at Defendants Cost
Ephraim Kennedy }

Henry Smerdon }
vs } Case
Peter Chastain }

I do hereby confess Judgment in the above case for the sum of ninety dollars and eighty two Cents with cost of suit. Peter Chastain 13 July 1797

Court adjourned till Saturday 10 o'clock. J. L. Dixon Dep. Clk.

Daniel McElduff }
vs } Detinue
Francis Coleman }

The plaintiff in this case within the time allowed by Law Issued an appeal and having complied with the terms of the Act, it was granted & William Coleman became his Security for the prosecution thereof in terms of the Law.

Saturday 15 July 1797. The Court met agreeably to adjournment.

Present Their Honors John Clements, Douglas Hancock, Solomon Woods, M. Shelman

Joseph Jackson who was appointed a Commissioner of the road leading from Vivions bridge to Louisville, having resigned. It is ordered that Joseph Bozeman be, and is hereby, appointed in lieu thereof.

Ordered, that in future, it shall be the mode of practice that parties be ruled to trial in all cases on the Issue Docket, on the first day of each Term, unless sufficient cause for its being continued.

It is ordered, that David Walker, be and he is hereby appointed Constable in Captain Parson's District, gave bond & Security & was qualified agreeably to Law.

It is Ordered, that William Flemming be and he is hereby appointed Overseer of the [38]
poor.

Ordered, that William McGohan, Chesley Bostwick, Sen., and William Flemming, be and they are hereby appointed Commissioners to act in conjunction with Zachariah Fenn, Peter Kolb, and Charles Coats, Esq., who were appointed to run a road from Fenns Bridge to Louisville, and report to this Court at the next meeting.

On the petition of Zachariah Lamar praying a license to retail Spirituous liquors. Ordered that the Clerk do issue license accordingly.

Ordered that James Stubbs, William McGehee, and John Paulett, be and are hereby [39]
appointed Inspectors of Tobacco at the Louisville Warehouse.

Charles Harvey, esquire, who was appointed Commissioner of the Road from Fenns bridge to Gates' Bridge suggesting his desire to resign, the Court granted it, and appointed Stephen Morgan in lieu of said Commissioner.

On the petition of Thomas Collier, &c praying a license to sell Spirituous Liquors in smaller quantities than one quart. Ordered that the Clerk do issue license agreeably to law.

On the petition of Messrs. Posner & Benedix praying to sell Spiritously liquors in smaller quantities than one quart. Ordered that the Clerk do issue license agreeably to law.

On the petition of Elijah Padgett praying to sell Spirituous liquors in smaller quantities than one quart. Ordered that the Clerk do issue license agreeably to law.

Ordered that the Clerk do pay Samuel Gates fifty dollars, in part for building a Bridge [40]
across Rocky Comfort at the place called Gates' Bridge.

Ordered that the Clerk do pay to Michael Shelman, esquire, one hundred dollars in part for.

Ordered that the Clerk do pay to Richard Gray, esquire, ninety eight dollars out of the first monies that may come into his hands arising from the present year tax.

The Court adjourned till the 25th day of this Month. Teste. J. L. Dixon, D. Clk. John Shellman, Duglass Hancock, John Clements, S. Wood, M. Shelman.

Tuesday, 25th July 1797 [41]

The Court met agreeably to adjournment. Present, Their Honors John Shelman, Douglass Hancock, M. Shelman, John Clements.

On the petition of Lindsay Coleman praying a License to retail Spirituous Liquors in Smaller quantities than one quart. Ordered, That the Clerk do issue License accordly.

On the petition of Manis Lemle praying a License to retail Spirituous Liquors by the Senales. Ordered, That the Clerk do issue License accordingly.

On the petition of John Barron praying a License to retail Spirituous Liquors by the Senales. [42]
Ordered, That the Clerk do issue License accordingly.

Ordered, that Jesse Womack be and he is hereby appointed a Commissioner to open a road from Nathaniel Samples' to the County line agreeably to a former Order of this Court in lieu of John Moreland , who has neglected to act.

Ordered, that the road leading from Louisville to Fenns Bridge (as directed by an order of this Court at December Term last) on the report of the joint Commissioners appointed to review said

Road be and is hereby directed to be opened as follows (viz) beginning at the West end of Sixth Street, running the most convenient course to Rocky Comfort Bridge, thence to Cobbs Pond, thence the new marked way to Vinings on the Long branch, thence the most direct & convenient way till it intersects the Augusta road near Fenns plantation.

On the petition of John Golding praying a License to retail Spirituous Liquors by the Senales.[43]
Ordered, that the Clerk issue a license accordingly.

Ordered, that the Clerk do take bond with sufficient Security in the sum of two hundred and fourteen dollars thirty cents of all persons applying for licenses to keep a tavern agreeably to an act of the General Assembly, passed the 24 December 1791.

Ordered that Samuel Gates be allowed a further sum of fifty dollars for building a Bridge across Rocky Comfort where Gates Bridge formerly stood.

The Court adjourned till 10 o'clock tomorrow.

Wednesday, 26 July 1797. The Court met according to adjournment. Present, John Clements, John Shelman, Douglass Hancock, M. Shelman, Justices of the Infr Court.

Ordered, that the Overseer of the Poor, pay to Sally Morgan, or order the sum of thirty [45]
dollars yearly, in quarterly payments of Seven Dollars and fifty Cents each, as soon as money may come into his hands.

Ordered, that the Clerk pay Samuel Gates the sum of fifty dollars as a second payment for building a Bridge across Rocky Comfort, according to a former order of this Court at July Term 1796.

Ordered, that all of the Inhabitants residing in Sixth Street, from the lower end to the Market house, including all on the South side thereof, liable to work on roads, shall be subject to work on the road to be opened, from Louisville to Powell's Bridge, across Ogechee, and that John Barron be and he is hereby appointed a Commissioner of said Road, in lieu of Thompson Lawson who refuses to act. And that John Downer be and he is hereby appointed an overseer from Louisville to Ogechee, & Seth Fountain be appointed Overseer from Ogechee to Boggy Gut, & Jacob Horn from Boggy Gut to the County line.

Ordered, that John Clements be and he is hereby appointed Guardian for Nancy Gibson [46]
Daughter of William Gibson decd that he give bond & Security in terms of the Law.

Ordered, that William Thomas, be and is hereby appointed Constable in the District of Louisville in lieu of John Mackey resigned.

Ordered, that William Herron, William Hadden, and James Young be and they are hereby appointed Commissioners to view and report the necessity & propriety of a Road from John Vinings, to John Donalsons, from thence to Philip Tippens', thence into the Augusta road near David Youngs, & report to this Court at the next Term.

Ordered, that Charles Harvey, esquire, is hereby authorized to take into his possession a certain natural son of Thomas Harvey and married Harvey French in consequence of his having complied with the Law in that case made & provided.

On Information, that Captain Tandy Key had in his possession a four shilling stamp (the [46]
date of which is 1779.) Ordered that he bring the same into Court, he accordingly did bring it in, and delivered it to the Court. Whereupon, it is Ordered that the Clerk deposit the same in the State Treasury, subject to the order of this Court, and take the Treasury's receipt for the same and file it of record.

Ordered, that Michael Shelman be paid a further sum of one hundred and fifty dollars in part for building a bridge across Rocky Comfort near Louisville.

Court adjourned till Court in Turn. J. L. Dixon, D. Clk. John Shellman, John Clements, Duglass Hancock, M. Shelman.

At an Inferior Court held in and for the County of Jefferson, at the House of Joseph Cheares, [47]
on Thursday the 7th December 1797. Present. Their Honors John Shelman, Duglass Hancock, M. Shelman, Esqrs.

Court adjourned till tomorrow 10 o'clock. Jas. Bozeman, Ck.

Friday 8th December 1797. Court met agreeably to adjournment. Present. Their Honors John Shelman, M. Shelman, Duglass Hancock, esquires.

Application having been made to the honorable, the Inferior Court of Jefferson County for [48]
the sale of a certain tract of land containing two hundred & fifty acres on Brushey Creek, the property of William Strother (deceased) and being duly advertised nine Months in Terms of the Act, and no person appearing to gainsay the sale.

On Motion of the Attorney for the administrator, It is ordered that the Rule be made absolute & the sale take place in terms of the act in such Case made & provided.

Ordered that the Collector do Collect one fourth of the Amount of the General Tax for the present year as a County Tax for the uses & purposes pointed out by the Tax Act and that the Clerk furnish the Collector with a Copy hereof and he is hereby directed to attend and Give Bond & Security as the law directs – previous to his Commencing his Collection of the same.

Application having been made to the Honorable, the Inferior Court of Jefferson County, for [49]
the sale of the real estate of Samuel McNeel, deceased, and being duly advertised nine Months in terms of the act and no person appearing to Gainsay the Sale. On Motion of the attorney for Daniel McNeel, administrator, It is Ordered that the Rule be made absolute & the sale take place in terms of the act in such Case made & provided.

It is ordered, that William Hadden, John Donaldson, and Philip Tippens, be and they are hereby appointed Commissioners to open a road from Captain John Vinings, near the Chickasaw fort on Duhart's Creek, to John Donaldsons, thence to Philip Tippens' on Brushey Creek, thence into the Augusta Road near David Youngs, agreeably to a report of William Herron & William Hadden.

Ordered that Hezekiah Gates be and he is hereby appointed Commissioner of the lower end [50]
of the road leading from Georgetown to Louisville.

On the petition of a number of Inhabitants praying an order for a road to be opened from Montgomery, where the County line intersects the Savannah road, from thence towards the White Ponds, also a road leading from where the Savannah road intersects the Hurricane, to the lower Bridge on Williamsons Swamp, and to Join the road leading from Louisville to Montgomery Court house at Boggy Gut.

It is ordered, that Joab Horn, Morris Raiford, & Elisha Nail be appointed Commissioners to view the ground on which the aforesaid roads are to run and report the propriety and necessity of opening said roads.

Ordered that the late Clerk of this Court pay into the hands of the present Clerk all the fees due the said Court as allowed by the Judiciary and that he be served with a copy hereof.

On the petition of Joseph Chears praying a License to Retail Spirituous liquors by the small. [51]
Ordered that the Clerk do Issue license and take Bond with sufficient Security according to law.

Mr. Jn° Parlett appeared and was Qualified as a deputy Sheriff for this County as the Law directs.

Ordered that William Cauthorn be and he is hereby appointed Overseer of the Road in Lieu of Joab Horn who has neglected to act on information of Stephen Powell one of the Commissioners.

Ordered that the Collector do immediately pay into the hands of the Clerk the County Tax that may be in his hands and furnish a True Statement of his Collection on or before the 23rd day of December Inst in order that appropriations may be made agreeably thereto, and that the Clerk do serve him with a Copy of this order.

Court adjourned till tomorrow 10 o'clock. Jas. Bozeman, Ck. [52]

Saturday, 9th December 1797. Court met agreeably to adjournment. Present, Their Honors, Duglass Hancock, Jno Shelman, Michael Shelman, esquires.

Ordered that the Clerk furnish M. Wm Hardwick, Receiver of Taxable Returns, with a Certificate from Under his hand for the Amount due him on the General & County Tax, at the Rate of Two and one half p. Centum, agreeably to the Tax Act.

On the petition of James and George House, praying the Court to appoint Robert House their [53]
Guardian. It is thereupon Ordered that the said Robert House be and he is hereby appointed guardian to the said James and George House, and that he attend and give bond and good and sufficient security for the faithful performance of duties of his Guardianship in terms of the Act in such cases made and provided.

On the petition of a number of Inhabitants praying a road from Louisville to James Roger's. It is therefore Ordered that a road be opened to Commence at the New road, near James Woodburns, thence the most convenient course to where the old road Crosses Harveys branch, thence till it intersects Major Barrien's line, thence along said line till it intersects John Shelmans line, thence to cross Grants Creek, where the old road crosses, thence up the said Creek in a parallel direction near said Shelman's back line, thence the most convenient way to where it intersects the new [54]
road, opened from Grays Mill to Philip Claytons, and that Blessingham Harvey, Senr, John Shelman, and John Barrien, be and they are hereby appointed Commissioners for opening and keeping in repair the said road.

On the information of Mr Wm Brackett. Ordered that Jno Parsons, Senr be and he is hereby appointed Commissioner of the Road leading from Louisville to Savannah in place of David Jamerson who has neglected to act.

Ordered that Saml Andrews and Jno Chastain be and they hereby appointed Commissioners of the Road leading from Louisville to Fenns Bridge in lieu of Peter Kolb & Shadrick Vining who have declined acting and that all the Inhabitants liable to work on public Roads shall open and keep in good Repair
said Road from the Sand hill Pond, as far as said Fenns bridge, who reside within the [55]
district formed by a direct line, drawn from said pond to the Ogechee River, then up the River to Fenns bridge, thence along the Road leading from said bridge to Gates, to where the old Bridge Road leads off, then down said Road to the aforesaid pond.

Ordered that the Clerk Give Notice to all persons who applied for license to retail Spirituous Liquors to attend and pay the money for the same on or before the 23 day of December Ins^{t}, otherwise they will be subject to the penalty of the Law.

On the application of Charles Gachet praying a license to retail spirituous liquors. It is ordered that the Clerk Issue license accordingly.

On the application of Jno Blair praying license to retail spirituous liquors in small quantities. It is ordered that the Clerk do issue them.

A list of Jurors drawn to serve at July term 1798 [56]

1. Saml Hammock
2. Wm C. Bond
3. Wm Vining
4. Jesse Skinner
5. Henry Harris
6. Jesse Cary
7. Wm Conner
8. S. Direzcaux
9. Jos. Hall
10. Danl Eubanks
11. Wm Donaldson
12. Thos Whitehead
13. Roger Smith
14. Ash Wood
15. Wm Peel
16. Arthur Herren
17. Henry Tucker
18. Wm Thompson
19. Solo. Willy, Junr
20. Richd Davis
21. Oren Watson
22. Saml Walden
23. Jno Davis
24. Wm Toakes
25. A. Carswell
26. Herman May
27. Jas. Weeks
28. S. Chance
29. Jos. Smith
30. Nathl Williams
31. Jas. Caldholn
32. Kensman Wright
33. Benj. Selvy
34. Jno Darby
35. Saml Ross
36. Jos. Parsons
37. Wm Parsons
38. Jas. Hall
39. Jno Parsons
40. Robt Little
41. Jno Green
42. Chas. Gates
43. Benj. Warner
44. Chas. Weeks
45. David Paulett
46. Jere Wilsher [57]
47. Jesse Hatcher
48. Wm Cannon

Court adjourned 23 Decr 1797. Test. Jas. Bozeman, Ck. Jno Shellman, Duglass Hancock, M. Shelman.

Saturday 23rd December 1797. Court met Agreeably to Adjournment. Present. Their Honors Jno Shelman, Duglass Hancock, Jno Clements, M. Shelman, esquires.

On the application of John Stringer, Senr. It is ordered that in consequence of his extreme Indigence that he be and is hereby freed from paying poll Tax. [58]

Ordered that William Caulthorn, Esq. be and is hereby appointed Commiss^{r} of the Road leading from Louisville to Woods bridge in the room of Wm Neel, resigned, and James Spivy is hereby appointed Overseer for said Road.

Ordered that thirty six Dollars & fifty Cents, being the amount of the County tax for the year 1795, be and is hereby appropriated for the express purpose of paying the claims now against the County of Burke for a Bridge Built across Rocky Comfort and Ogechee River so far as the above amt. of 36.50 and no more, and the Clerk be authorized to pay
the same as soon as such monies may come into his hands agreeably to the above order. [59]

The Tax Collector appeared and laid before the Court a Statement of the County Tax and a partial settlement was made thereon. Ordered that he do pay into the hands of the Clerk such monies as are still due as fast as he may be able to Collect the same, in order that the respective claims against the County may be discharged as soon as possible and that he, be prepared to make a final settlement the ensuing term.

Court adjourned till Court in course. [60]
Test. Jas. Bozeman, Ck. Jno. Shellman, Duglass Hancock, M. Shelman.

March 7th 1798. Agreeably to an act past in the year 1796, the Justices of the Inferior Court met for the purpose of appointing the Collector of Taxes & Receiver of Tax Returns.

Present Jno Clements, Jno Shelman, M. Shelman, Esquires

Ordered that Duglass Hancock be and is hereby appointed Collector for the year 1798, that William Hardwick be and is hereby appointed receiver of Tax returns for the year 1798.

Test. Jas Bozeman, Clk. John Clements, Jno Shellman, M. Shelman.

Georgia } At an Inferior Court held in and for the County aforesaid [61]
Jefferson County } on the 11th day of July 1798

Present their Honors John Shelman, Solo. Wood, Mich^{l} Shelman, Jno Clements, esquires, Justices of the said Court.

Jurors Called and Sworn.

Jury N° 1

1. Saml Hammack
2. Wm C. Bond
3. Jesse Cary
4. Simpson Chance
7. Thomas Whitehead
8. Ashley Wood
9. Isaac Coleman
10. Jno Davis

5. Joseph Hall
6. Wm Donaldson
11. Hermin May
12. James Weeks

Court adjourned till tomorrow 9 o'clock. Jas. Bozeman, Clk.

Thursday, the 12th July court met agreeably to adjournment. [62]

Present their Honors Jno Shelman, Duglass Hancock, Jno Clements, Solo. Wood, Michl Shelman, Esquires

Jno Woods, assignee }
of Wm Daniel }
vs } Covenant
Frederick Clem }

Jury No 1

1. Saml Hammack
2. Wm C. Bond
3. Jesse Cary
4. Simpson Chance
5. Joseph Hall
6. Wm Donaldson
7. Thos Whitehead
8. Ashley Wood
9. Isaac Coleman
10. Jno Davis
11. Herman May
12. James Weeks

We find for the Plaintiff Seventy eight Dollars with cost of suit. James Coleman, foreman

Elizabeth Palmer } [63]
vs } Case
David Douglass }

In this case, the Defendant came into Court and acknowledged himself bound to the plaintiff in the sum of two hundred Dollars. William Boon at the same time acknowledged himself bound to the plaintiff in a like sum of two hundred Dollars on the condition following. That the defendant in this suit should pay the eventual condemnation money, surrender himself in discharge thereof, or that the said William Boon should sit for him. David Douglass, William Boon

John Tenns }
vs } Spl. Case
I. McElduff }

Isaac Coleman, who was one of the bail, came into Court and paid the cost of the suit upon the Bail Bond and him together with Wm Coleman entered Special Bail in the words following: We Isaac Coleman, of the County of Jefferson, Planter, and William Coleman, of the same place, planter, acknowledge ourselves jointly and severally bound to John Townsen the sum of twelve

hundred Dollars, on the Condition that if the Defendant shall be cast in the suit, he the Defendant Dan[l] McElduff will pay the condemnation money, surrender himself as the Law directs, or we will do it for him. Taken [64]
and acknowledged before me in open Court. Is[c] Coleman W[m] Coleman

Test. Jas. Bozeman

Jn[o] Towns }
vs } Special Case
Dan[l] McElduff }

Witneses Sworn: James George, David Hardridge

2nd Jury

1. Natha[l] Williams	7. William Parsons
2. Solo. Willy	8. David Paulett
3. Jas. Parsons	9. Tho[s] Peebles
4. Jas. Hall	10. Joseph Smith
5. Jn[o] Parsons	11. W[m] Manson
6. Benj. Warner	12. Rich[d] Parker

We find no cause of action against Daniel McElduff. Jas. Parson, foreman

William Stone } [65]
vs } Case
R. E. Randolph }

In this case, the Defendant came into Court and acknowledged himself bound to the plaintiff in the sum of sixty three dollars & fifty six and one half Cents. Abner Hammond at the same time acknowledged himself bound to the plaintiff in a like sum of sixty three dollars & fifty six cents on the condition following. That the defendant in this suit should pay the eventual condemnation money, surrender himself in discharge thereof, or that the said Abner Hammond should do it for him. Rich[d] Randolph Abner Hammond

Jas. Bozeman, Clk.

I. Bostick, Jun[r] } [66]
vs } Case
Henry Shafer }

1. Sam[l] Hammack	7. Tho[s] Whitehead
2. W[m] C. Bond	8. Ashley Wood
3. Jesse Cary	9. Isaac Coleman

4. Simpson Chance | 10. Jn° Davis
5. Joseph Hall | 11. Herman May
6. Wm Donaldson | 12. Jas. Weeks

We find a verdict for the Plaintiff for one hundred and seventeen dollars and 87½ cents.
Isaac Coleman, foreman

Zachariah Henderson }
vs } Case
Horatio Marburay } Witness Wm Thompson

Same Jury as before. We find no cause of action against the defendant. Is^{c} Coleman, foreman

Tubman, Petty & Tubman } [67]
vs } Case
Zachariah Gray }

I do hereby confess Judgment for sum of seventy five dollars and 72 Cents with cost of suit.
Zachariah Gray, July Term 1798

Jn° Bostick & Co. }
vs } Case
Zachariah Gray }

I do hereby confess Judgment for the Sum of one hundred and twenty seven dollars and thirty five and three q^{r} Cents with cost. Zach^{r} Gray, July Term 1798

Christopher Brooks } [68]
vs } Case
John Shellman }

I do hereby appear in Court and confess Judgment to Christopher Brooks for the sum of two hundred dollars principle, and thirty eight dollars Interest, with cost of suit, with three Months stay of levy. July 12th 1798. Jn° Shellman

Court adjourned till tomorrow morning 9 o'clock. Jas. Bozeman, Clk.
Jn° Shellman, Duglass Hancock, John Clements, Solomon Wood

Friday, the 13th July, the Court met agreeably to adjournment. [69]

Present, their Honors Jn° Shelman, Douglass Hancock, Solomon Woods, Jn° Clements, Esquires

William Jenkins }
vs } Trover
Michael Shelman }

Jurors Sworn

1. Natha[l] Williams	7. William Parsons
2. Solo. Willy	8. David Paulett
3. Jas. Parsons	9. Tho[s] Peebles
4. Jas. Hall	10. Joseph Smith
5. Jn[o] Parsons	11. W[m] Manson
6. Benj. Warner	12. Rich[d] Parker

No cause of action against Michael Shelman. Jas. Parsons, foreman

Theary Croely, asse } [70]
vs } Case
Henry G. Caldwell }

Jurors sworn

1. Sam[l] Hammack	7. Tho[s] Whitehead
2. W[m] C. Bond	8. Ashley Wood
3. Jesse Cary	9. Isaac Coleman
4. Simpson Chance	10. Jn[o] Davis
5. Joseph Hall	11. Herman May
6. W[m] Donaldson	12. Jas. Weeks

We find for the Plaintiff fifty three dollars and 45 Cents, which is the principle and Interest, with Cost of Suit. Isaac Coleman, foreman

Jn[o] & M. Shelman }
vs } Debt
Zachariah Gray }

I do hereby confess Judgment for the Sum of five hundred and fifty one dollars & 50 Cents with cost of suit. Stay of levy until the 25th day of October next. Zachariah Gray

James Bennett } [71]
vs } Non Suit
Matthias Dalton }

George Walker, ass[ee] }
vs } Case
Posner & Benedix }

Judgment confessed for the sum of five hundred and fifty seven dollars and thirty cents and cost of suit, with a stay of levy five months, upon giving security for the payment of the money at that time. Posner & Benedix. 13 July 1798

Isaac Chance }
vs } Debt
Jno Styron } Dismissed at the Plaintiffs Cost.

Thomas Wray }
vs } Case
William Evans } Dismissed at the Plffs Cost

Jno Scraggs } [72]
vs } Case
Jesse Paulett } Dismissed at the Plaintiff Cost

George Prince }
vs } Attachment
Jno Cawdle } Dismissd for Irregularity

Court adjourned till tomorrow Morning 9 o'clock. Jas. Bozeman, Clk. Jno Shellman, Duglass Hancock, John Clements, Solomon Wood

Saturday, the 14th July 1798. [73]
Cout met agreeably to adjournment. Present, their Honors Duglass Hancock, Solo. Wood, Michael Shelman, Jno Clements, Jno Shelman

James Harvey }
vs } Case
Jno Caudle & }
Henry Abbott }

1. Samuel Hammack	7. Thos Whitehead
2. Wm C. Bond	8. Ashley Wood
3. Jesse Cary	9. Isaac Coleman
4. Simpson Chance	10. Jno Davis
5. James Manson	11. Herman May
6. Wm Donaldson	12. Jas. Weeks

We find for the Plaintiff eighty five dollars and seventy four cents, with cost of suit.
Isaac Coleman, foreman

William Jenkins } [74]
vs } Trover
Michael Shelman }

The Plaintiff in this case, within the time allowed by law, claimed an appeal and having complid with the terms of the act, it was granted and Jesse Thomas became his Security for the prosecution thereof in terms of the Law. Wm Jenkins Jesse Thomas

Solomon Wood }
vs } Case
Jno Golding }

I do hereby confess Judgment for the sum of eighty six dollars and cost of suit, stay of levy nine months. John Golding, July term 1798

Brittain McCullers } [75]
vs } Slander
Mathias Dalton } Nonsuch

Brittain McCullers }
vs } Case
Mathias Dalton } Nonsuch

~~John M. Whitney }~~
~~vs } Attachment~~
~~George N. Rangan }~~

~~1. Jesse Cary~~
~~2. Wm Donaldson~~
~~3. Thos Whitehead~~

Upon the return of a Habeas corpus, issued at the instance of Ephraim Peebles, who was confined in the common Jail on a Casa at the Suit of Jacob Whitehead, the following Schedule of all the property belonging to the said Ephraim Peebles of the County of Jefferson was exhibited to the Court.

A note of hand, given by one John Raines who formerly resided in Savannah, dated the 28th [76]
day of may 1784, for a likely young negroe, one ditto from Benjamin Guess Indorsed by said Raines for a negroe dated the 3rd of May 1785.

Whereupon, the said Ephraim Peebles took the following oath in open Court, to wit. I Ephraim Peebles do solemnly swear in the presence of almighty god that I am not possessed of any real or personal estate, debts, Credits, or effects whatsoever, my wearing apparel, beding for myself and

family, and the working tools and implements of my trade and calling excepted, wherewith to maintain and support myself during my imprisonment that are contained in this Schedule, now [illegible] and that I have not directly or indirectly since my imprisonment or before sold, assigned, or otherwise disposed of or made over in trust for myself or otherwise any part of my lands, estate, goods, Stock, money, debts, or other real or personal estate whereby to have any benefit or profit to myself or my heirs, so help me god.
Ephraim X Peebles [his mark]

And it not appearing to the Court that there is any fraud in the act or manner of these Peebles in this regard.
Order that the said Ephraim Peebles be and he is hereby enlarged, discharged, and set at Liberty. [77]

Court adjourned till Friday, the 20th July Inst Test. Jas. Bozeman, Clk. Jno Shellman, Solomon Wood, Duglass Hancock, M. Shelman, John Clements

John Towns }
vs } Special case
Danl McElduff }

The Plaintiff in this case, within the time allowed by law, claimed and appeal, and having compled with the terms of the act, it was granted and Wm Towns became his Security for the prosecution thereof in terms of the Law. Wm Towns

Theary Croeley, asse } [78]
vs } Case
Henry G. Caldwell }

The defendant in this case within the time allowed by law claimed an appeal and having complied with the terms of the act, it was granted, and Eli Browning became his Security for the Prosecution thereof in terms of the Law. Hy Caldwell. Eli Browning.

Jno Woods, asse of }
William O'Daniel }
vs } Case
Fred. Clem }

In this case, the defendant came into this Office and Wm McGehee and bound themselves Jointly to the Plaintiff for the amount of the verdict, for Stay of execution sixty days. July 17th 1798.
Fred Clem William McGehee

Friday, the 20th July 1798 [79]

The Court met agreeably to adjournment. Present, their Honors John Shelman, Duglass Hancock, Solomon Wood, Jn° Clements, M. Shelman, Esquires.

This day, came into Court John L. Dixon, the late Deputy Clerk of this Court and paid the full amount of the Court fees on all suits commenced by him in the years 1796 and 1797.

Ordered that John L. Dixon, esqr., Clerk of the Superior Court, do come into court and render an account of all monies now in his hands, which has arisen from the sales of estrays.

William P. Allen was appointed Constable for Captain Vinings district and was qualified according to Law.

Ordered that a road be opened from the Hurricane on the County line to the lower Bridge on Wmson swamp, from thence the nearest and most convenient way to Louisville, and that Stephen Powell, Morris Raiford, & John Cowart, be and they are hereby appointed Commissioners, Surveyors, and overseers for opening and keeping in repair said Roads, and the road leading from Louisville to Montgomery Court House, and that they and a majority of them are hereby particularly author[illegible] to order out for opening, and working on said Roads, all the hands belonging to Captain Morris Raifords district who are subject to such service. And that such of the Inhabitants of Louisville and its Vicinity mentioned in an order of the 26 July 1797 be and are hereby subject to work on said Roads, as is therein expressed.

Ordered that where it shall so happen that hands subject to work on roads, do refuse or neglect to attend,
when warned thereto, it shall and may be the duty of the Commissioners &c and they are [81]
hereby authorized to hire hands to work in their stead, and pay them with the money collected as a penalty from the delinquents agreeably to the law, in that case made and provided. And, the Clerk is hereby directed to furnish each of the Commissioners with a copy of this order.

Ordered that Samuel Benedix be and he is hereby appointed Commissioner of the road leading from Louisville to James Rogers's in the room of Jn° Shelman, esqr., resigned.

Ordered that Elijah Padget, Duett Dees, and Simon Smith be and they are hereby appointed Overseers for keeping in repair the road leading from Louisville to Vivions Bridge on Wmsons swamp, from thence to the County line, and the said overseers are hereby authorized to divide the hands, and cause them to work on said road as they may think proper and most advantagious.

Ordered that the Clerk do pay Michael Shelman a further sum of eighty dollars for building [82]
the Bridge across Rocky Comfort, the payment or payments to be proportioned agreeably to the respective Claims against the County.

Ordered that John Paulett be and is hereby appointed to receive and take the Census in Major Caldwells Battalion, and Chesley Bostick, Senr for Major Scotts Battalion.

Court adjourned till tomorrow 9 o'Clock. Jas, Bozeman, Clk.

Saturday, the 21st July 1798. Court met agreeably to adjournment. Present Jno Shelman, Mich^{l} Shelman, Solo. Wood, Esquires

A list of Jurors drawn to serve at December Term 1798 [83]

1. John Parker
2. Robt Brady
3. Aquilla Low
4. Mich. Calhoon
5. Jno McMahan
6. Adam Cahoon
7. W^{m} McBride
8. David Shores
9. Jno Thompson
10. Henry Land
11. Wm Kennedy
12. Alex Avery
13. Jno Mathews
14. Benj. Perkins
15. Thomas Wotton
16. Thomas Little
17. Headen Tilman
18. Joseph Allen
19. Jno Foyl
20. Thompson Lawson
21. Wm Boon
22. Jacob Godown
23. Saml Little
24. Robert Fleming
25. Peter Mathews
26. Jno Greene
27. Thos McBride, Junr
28. Wylle Adkins
29. Jno Tinsley
30. Wm Leaton
31. W^{m} McGlohan
32. Elkanah Briggs
33. Fred. Evans
34. Hered Dupree
35. Thomas Kennedy
36. Abram Lafavour
37. Robert Prior
38. David Brinson
39. Stephen Morgan
40. And. Bush
41. Jno Cuning
42. Roger Lawson
43. Andrew Berrihill, Senr
44. Jacob Young
45. Jno Sandafer
46. Peter McCarter
47. Wm Dassy
48. Thomas Parsons

Ordered that the overseer of the poor do pay to Thomas Duglas, Jno Stringer, and Nancy [84] Neel, the sum of Thirty dollars each, yearly or quarterly payments of seven dollars & fifty Cents each, as soon as money shall come into his hands.

William Vining, Jesse Hatcher, Samuel Walden, Jno Darby, Daniel Eubanks, Robert Little, James Calhoon, and Allen Carswell, having been duly summoned to attend this term as Jurors, and their names being called, did make default.

It is ordered that they be fined in the sum of five dollars each, unless they should shew good and sufficient cause of excuse by an affidavit to be made before some Justice of the Peace and file the same with the Clerk of this Clerk on or before the first day of the next term, the 7th Decr 1798. And that this rule be published four weeks successively that the said deponents may have due notice thereof.

Ordered that the Clerk do pay to John Paulett , late Sheriff, the sum of Twenty one dollars [85]
and twenty five Cents of the County tax for the present year, as soon as the same may come into his hands.

William Cook came into court and of his own free will and accord appointed the Court his Guardian and accordingly Indented himself to William Wilson for the term of six years, agreeably to the Indenture filed in the Clerks office.

Epsey Wallace came into Court and of her own free will and accord appointed the Court her Guardian and accordingly Indented herself to Joseph White for the term of four years, agreeably to the Indenture filed in the Clerks office.

Ordered that the late Collector attend on Saturday the 4th day of august next at the Court house in Louisville prepared to account fully with the Court for all the monies Collected by him as a County Tax, during the time for which he was appointed, and in case of his refusing

or neglecting to attend, execution shall issue against him in terms of the act. [86]

Ordered, That thirty dollars be paid to Tandy C. Key, out of the thirty six dollars appropriated for paying the Claims against Burk County for Building Bridges by persons with this County in part of his the said Keys Claim and six dollars & fifty Cents to the heirs of David Ward, Senr, deceased, in part of his Claim.

Ordered that the sum of Ten dollars be paid to Joseph Chears for each Term that has or may hereafter be held in the House belonging to said Chears, out of the Funds arising from the County Tax, to be paid by the Clerk, as soon as money May come into his hands.

Ordered that one fourth of the General Tax be levied for the use of the County, and likewise the two and thirteenth part of said General Tax, to pay the arrearages of Fees due to the Sheriff and Jailer as allowed by law.

Ordered that those persons who made application for license for retailing spirituous liquors [87]
at the terms of July & December 1797 and did not comply with the terms of the act, do attend at the Clerks office of this Court and pay the Tax due on the same, on or before the 4th day of August next, and in case of refusal or neglect, they will be proceeded against agreeably to law.

Ordered that Thomas Fulton be and is hereby appointed a Justice of the Peace, for the district of Captain Parsons, and that a Copy of this order be transmitted to the Executive department.

Ordered that William Herren be and is hereby appointed a Commissioner of a Road leading from Captain Vinings to Philip Tippenses, thence into the Augusta Road near David Youngs, in the room of Philip Tippens resigned.

Court adjourned till the fourth day of August next, 10 o'Clock. Jas. Bozeman, Crk. Jn° Shellman, John Clements, Solomon Wood, M. Shelman

On the petition of Alexander Love praying a license to retail spirituous liquors in a less [88]
Quantity than one quart. It is ordered that the Clerk do issue thence and take bond & security agreeably to the Act in such cases made & provided.

On the petition of Levy D. Smith praying a license to retail spirituous liquors in a less Quantity than one quart and to keep a Tavern in the Town of Louisville. It is ordered that the Clerk do issue license and take bond with good security agreeably to the Act in such Cases made & provided.

The Court then proceeded to the Election of a Clerk for the Court of Ordinary, And on counting the Votes it appears that William McDowell was duly Elected.

Georgia } [89]
Jefferson County } At an Inferior Court began and held in and for the County aforesaid on the Seventh day of December 1798.

Present, their honors John Shelman, John Clements, Duglass Hancock, Esquires.

Robert Wilson }
vs } Trover
George Ingram } Nonsuit

Jurors called and sworn

1. Jacob Godown	7. David Shores
2. Abra. Lafavor	8. Fred^k Evans
3. John Thompson	9. Robert Pior
4. Peter Mathews	10. John Cuning
5. Dav^d Brinson	11. John Foil
6. Jacob Young	12. Thos Parsons

Philip Clayton } [90]
vs } Case
Zachariah Gray }

In this case, the defendant came into court and acknowledged himself bound in the sum [illegible] for, and William Allen appeared and acknowledged himself bound for the same sum, if Zachariah Gray should be cast therein, pay the eventual condemnation money, or render the body of the defendant in discharge thereof.

Posner & Benedix }
vs } Case
David Terry }

David Jamison came into court and entered himself special bail for the defendant in the above case, to pay the eventual condemnation money thereof, in case he shall be cast therein, or render the defendant in discharge thereof.

Court adjourned till tomorrow morning Ten O'Clock. Jas. Bozeman, Clk.

Saturday, the 3th December 1798. [91]

Court met agreeably to adjournment. Present, the Honorable Michael Shelman, Jn° Shelman, Jn° Clements, Judges of the same Court.

Same jury as before.

Morgan Minton }
vs } Special Case
George Weatherby }
& John Cobbs }

We find for the Plaintiff fifty two dollars & fifty Cents. Rob[t] Pior, Foreman

E. Palmer, Admin. }
vs } Case
David Duglass }

The Plaintiff made Nonsuit.

Court Adjourned till Monday 1 o'Clock. Jas. Bozeman, Clk.

Monday, 10th December 1798. Court met agreeably to Adjournment. Present, the Honorable Jn° Shelman, M. Shelman, D. Hancock, esquires.

Rich[d] Dickenson }
vs } Case
Pat. F. Carr }

Same Jury as before. We find for the Plaintiff the sum of eighty five doll. & 75 Cents. Rob[t] Pior, foreman

David Jamison }
vs } Case
Jacob Peterson } [93]

David Jamison and Jacob Peterson having deferred to us, the adjustment of a disagreement which has taken place between them relative to the hire of a horse. We are of opinion that Jacob Peterson ought to pay David Jamison the sum of eight dollars as a compensation for the said Horse. And also the cost incurred in consequence of a suit commenced therein.

Dan[l] Sturges Thomas Johnson

Robert Glasster }
vs } Attachment
Mathew Allbrittain } Dismissed at the Plaintiffs Cost

William Stone }
vs } Case
Rich[d] Randolph } Dismissed at the Plaintiffs Cost

Isaac Perry, et al } [94]
Commissioners of }
Burke Academy }
vs } Case
Jn[o] L. Dixon, }
Jn[o] Cobbs & A. Foos }

1. Herod Dupree	7. Jn[o] Downer
2. And. Bush	8. Tho[s] Neely
3. Rich[d] Paulett	9. Arth. Dupree
4. Young Beckham	10. Tho[s] Peebles
5. Charles Rhodes	11. William Thompson
6. Geo. Jones	12. Sam[l] Gates

We find for the Plaintiff two hundred and forty dollars with Interest from the Seventeenth day of Jan[y] 1798 and Cost, it being the first stallment due upon the bond declared on. Charles Rhodes, foreman

Tho[s] Carr }
vs } Case
Jn[o] Cobbs }

1. Jacob Godown	7. Dav^{d} Shores
2. A. Lafavor	8. Fred. Evans
3. Jno Thompson	9. Robt Pior
4. Pet. Mathews	10. Jno Cuning
5. Dav^{d} Brinson	11. Jno Foil
6. Jacob Young	12. Thos Parsons

We find for the Plaintiff six hundred dollars eighty three dollars & 32 Cents, interest included.
Robt Pior, foreman

Nathaniel Durkee } [95]
vs } Case
Jno Cobbs & G. Naylor }

1. Herod Dupree	7. Jno Downer
2. And. Bush	8. Thos Neely
3. Richd Paulett	9. A. Dupree
4. Young Beckham	10. Thos Peebles
5. Chas. Rhodes	11. Wm Thompson
6. Geo. Jones	12. Saml Gates

We find for the Plaintiff four hundred Dollars, with Interest from the 6th Octr 1797 to the 10th Decr 1798, with Cost of Suit. Charles Rhodes, foreman

Jno Richardson }
vs } Case
William Stone }

Same Jury as in the case of Thos Carr vs Jno Cobbs.

We find for the Plaintiff forty one Dollars & fifty Cents with Cost of Suit. Robt Pior, foreman

Joseph Miller } [96]
vs } Case
Zach^{r} Gray }

I do hereby appear in Court and confess Judgment unto Joseph Miller, the Plaintiff, for the sum of two hundred & sixteen dollars & 48 Cents, with Cost. Decr 9th 1798. Receipt from John Berrien as in full of the above Judgment. Zach Gray

Cr by John Barriens receipt for $110.00.

Rob[t] Dennis }
vs } Case
Posner & Benedix }

John Scott and William McDowell came into Court (with the defendants) and entered Special bail for the defendants in the above Case, to pay the eventual condemnation Money, in case the defendants be cast therein, or render the defendants in discharge thereof.

John Barrien } [97]
vs } Special Case
Thomas Johnson } Bail Discharged

Court Adjourned till tomorrow morning 10 O'Clock. Jas. Bozeman, Clk.

Tuesday Morning, 11th Decr 1798. Court met agreeably to Adjournment. Present, the Honorable Jn[o] Shelman, M. Shelman, Jn[o] Clements, esquires.

Posner & Benedix }
vs }
Jesse Paulett }

Tandy C. Key came into Court with the def[t] and ent[d] himself special bail, for the above case [98]
to pay the eventual condemnation money, in case he shall be cast therein, or render the defendant in discharge thereof.

Posner & Benedix } [98]
vs } case
Jesse Paulett }

I Jesse Paulette do appear in Court and confess a Judgment for the sum of two hundred and thirty eight Dollars, Eighty one & ¼ Cents, with Interest & Cost, with stay of Execution twelve Months. 11th Dec[r] 1798. Jess Paulett

Nathan Powell }
vs } Case
Jn[o] Golding }

Morris Gilbert and Jn[o] J. Schley came into Court with the defendant and ent[d] themselves special bail for the def[t] in the above Case, to pay the Eventual condemnation money should the he be cast therein, or render the body of the defendant in discharge thereof.

Posner & Benedix } [99]
vs } case
Jn° Paulett }

I do hereby confess Judgment for the Sum of two hundred & eighty five Dollars, Seventy one and three quarter Cents, with Interest & Cost in the above case with stay of Execution two years. Jn° Paulett

Jn° Shellman, M. Shelman, John Clements, J. C.

Thomas Carr }
vs } Case
Jn° Cobbs }

The defendant in this case, within the time allowed by law, claimed an appeal & having complied with the terms of the act, it was granted and Chesley Bostick, Junior became his security for the Prosecution thereof in terms of the law. 11 Dec[r] 98. John Cobbs C. Bostick, Jun[r]

Friday, 28th December 1798. [100]

Court met agreeably to adjournment. Present, the Honorable Jn° Clements, Jn° Shelman, Solo. Wood, Mich[l] Shelman, Judges of the said Court.

Ordered that the Clerk furnish William Hardwick, Esquire, receiver of Tax returns, with a certificate from under his hand, for the amount due him on the General and County tax, at the rate of Two and one half p. Centum, Agreeably to the tax act.

Ordered, That James Hunt, Alexander Love, and Jn° Foil, be and they are hereby appointed Commissioners of the road leading from Chickasaw Bridge on Brian Creek, to Louisville, so far as big Creek, And Henry G. Caldwell Commissioner of the said road, from the said big Creek to Louisville.

Ordered, that John Cobbs, William McGehee, and Michael Shelman be authorized to cause [101]
Tandy C. Key to lay before them, the original Contract for Building and keeping in repair the Bridge across the Rocky Comfort Creek, as also the amount by him received from the Inferior Court of Burke County, and that he do comply with the said Contract by puting in a good [illegible] and keep in repair the Bridge for the full Term expressed in his Obligation, which said Obligation be filed in the Clerks office of this Court, and the said Commissioners be authorized to draw on the Clerk for the balance due the said Key on the original contract, on his complying therewith. Otherwise, they are hereby directed to contract with some person, for puting in good repair the aforesaid Bridge, by letting the same to the lowest bidder, and that they do draw on the

Clerk for the sum the same may be let for, either for part or the whole of the Balance due the said Key.

Ordered, That Michael Shelman be allowed the sum of one hundred dollars, as a [102]
consideration for the Bridge across Ogechee River, known & called Shelmans Bridge & he do give Bond and Security, for putting & keeping in good repair the said Bridge for the term of Two years from this date, which bond the Clk is hereby authorized to take, and also pay the aforesaid one hundred Dollars out of any money that may come into his hands.

Ordered, That the Clerk do make out a true Statement of the fees due to the members of the Court and to pay to them respectively the sums due them when called on.

Court adjourned till the Eleventh of Jany 1799. Jas. Bozeman, Clk. M. Shelman, John [103]
Clements, Jno Shellman, Solomon Wood.

Friday, 11th January 1799. Court met agreeably to adjournment. Present, the Honorable Jno Clements, Jno Shelman, ~~M. Shelman~~, Solo. Wood.

Om Motion of Peter J. Carnes, attorney for the Plaintiffs in the following cases. [104]

Jno & M. Shelman }
vs }
Zachariah Gray }

Jno Bostwick & Co. }
vs }
Zachariah Gray }

Tubman, Petty & Tubman }
vs }
Zachariah Gray }

Ordered, That the Sheriff do Shew cause at 10 O'Clock tomorrow, why he does not return the Executions in the above cases, or why an attachment should not issue against him in Case of his failure to make return. The Court Adjourned till tomorrow 10 O'Clock. Jas. Bozeman, Clk.

Saturday, 12th January 1799. Court met agreeably to adjournment. Present, their Honors [105]
Jno Shelman, Jno Clements, Mich^{l} Shelman, Esquires.

1. Jno Darby
2. Jesse W. Mullen
3. Jas. Hall
4. Abner Adams

21. Elk Brigs
22. W. Whitaker
23. Robert Maxwell
24. Wm Caulthorn

45. Tho. Lawson
46. Robt Stone
47. Z. Gray
48. Solo. Willy

5. Wm Fountain
6. Ridden Hall
7. Jas. Harvey
8. Saml Ross
9. Jere Welcher
10. Jno Green
11. J^{as} McMahan
12. M. Calhon
13. Thos Harvey, Junr
14. William McBride
15.Wm Baker
16. Jno Ford
17. Jno Blair
18. Walter Graham
19. Stephen Morgan
20. Wm Parsons

25. Wm Boon
26. Saml Maho
27. Paoli Hall
28. Joab Horn
29. Jno Donalson
30. Jas. Neely
32. Wm Young
33. Jno Dupree
34. Ben Warner
35. Jno Denson
36. Reub. Ross
37. A. Avery
38. Jas. Smith
39. Benj. Acock
40. Wm Leggett
41. Wm Vining
42. Jona Fountain
43. Joseph Hall
44. Wm Spiers

Court Adjourned till Monday Morning 10 O'Clock. Test. Jas. Bostick, Clk. Jno Shellman, [106] John Clements, M. Shelman

Monday, 14th January 1799. Court met Agreeably to Adjournment. Present, their Honors Solomon Wood, Jno Clements, Duglass Hancock.

On the application of Jno Tanmer, Senior. It is ordered that in consequence of his extreme indigence that he be and is hereby freed from paying his poll Tax.

Ordered, That Duglass Hancock do pay to Joseph Shears Ten dollars on account of Court House rent.

Ordered, That the Clerk be authorized to make a Settlement with Mr. Jethro B. Spivy and [107] give him an order for the Money he has overpaid on the Collector of Taxes for the year 1798.

Court adjourned till court in course. Jas. Bozeman, Clk. Jno Shellman, John Clements, Duglass Hancock

On the Petition of John Black praying a license to retail Spirituous liquors in less quantities [108] than one quart. It is ordered that the Clerk do issue license and take Bond for the same. February 1st 1799.

The 11th July 1798. Present, the Honbles John Shelman, John Clements, Michael Shelman, [109] Duglass Hancock, Solomon Wood

Charles Gachett, James Bayard Chattien, and James G. Berkhoff Applied to the Court for admittance to Citizenship and having proved to the satisfaction of the Court that they were intitled to it, by the act of congress passed the twenty ninth day of January on thousand Seven hundred and ninety five, they were duly admitted and took the Oath prescribed by the said act.

Saturday, 16th March 1799. Present, the Honorable Thacker Vivion, John Clements, Michl [110] Shelman, Duglass Hancock, Richd Gray

ordered, that Robert Fullwood be and he is hereby appointed Receiver of tax returns for the year one thousand Seven hundred ninety nine.

Ordered, that Garland Hardwick be and is hereby appointed Collector of Taxes for the year one thousand Seven hundred & ninety nine.

Ordered, that Douglass Hancock, esquire, Collector of the taxes for the year one thousand Seven hundred & ninety eight do pay into the hands of the Clerk of this Court, the County tax of the said year.

Test. Jas. Bozeman, Clk. R. D. Gray, M. Shelman, John Clements, Thack Vivion [111]

Georgia. In conformity to an act of the General Assembly of this State, passed the 16th day of February one thousand seven hundred and ninety nine, entitled and act to compell all officers, Civil & Military to take and subscribe an Oath to support the Constitution thereof.

Comes William McDowell, esquire, Clerk of the Superior Court of the County of Jefferson, took and Subscribed the Oath required by the said act, in the words following, to wit. I, William McDowell, do Solemnly Swear that I will bear true faith and allegiance to the State of Georgia and to the upmost of my Power & ability, observe, conform to, support and defend the Constitution thereof without any reservation or equivocation Whatsoever and the Constitution of the United States, So help me God. Taken before me 22 Mar 99. Wm. McDowell, Clk Superior Court. Jas. Bozeman, Clk.

Monday, April 1st 1799. [112]

Pursuant to a Joint Resolution of the General Assembly passed the 16th day of February 1799 for nominating Justices of the peace in each Captains district agreeably to the fifth section of the third article of the Constitution, the justices of the Inferior Court met, and proceeded to make the following Nominations, to wit.

for Captain Vinings district, William Hardwick & John Vining for Captain Terrys district, Robert Patterson & Daniel Connel

for Captain Hamptons district, Joseph Hampton & John Whitehead

for Captain Carswells district, Benj. Whitaker & A. Hammond

for Captain Johnsons district, Horatio Marbury & J. Merewether

for Captain Tarvers district, John Raiford & Wm Clements [113]

for Captain Raifords district, Wm Cauthorn & John Woods

for Captain Vivions district, Thacker Vivion, Junr & Robt Fullwood

for Captain Keys district, Charles Runnels & Hezekiah Gates

and they are hereby severally Nominated as Justices of the Peace for the respective districts.

Attest. Jas. Bozeman, Clk. M. Shelman, Thac^{k} Vivion, John Clements, R. D. Gray, Duglass Hancock

ordered that the Clerk do transmit a copy of the aforegoing appointments to the Executive agreeable to the aforesaid resolution.

Georgia [104]
In conformity to an act of the General Assembly of this State, passed the 16th day of February 1799, entitled an act to compell all officers civil and Military to take and Subscribe an Oath to Support the Constitution thereof. Came the following Subscribers and took the Oath required by the said act in the words following, to wit.

We do Solemnly Swear that we will bear true faith and allegiance to the State of Georgia and to the utmost of our power and abilities observe, conform to, support, and defend the constitution thereof, without any reservation or equivocation whatsoever; and the constitution of the United States, so help me God.

Tho. Fulton
22 Jany 1803
Geo. R. Clayton
Ens^{n} of the Louisville
[illegible] Guards
11th Feby 1803

M. O. A. Johnson

Captn Louis Wittcomb Jefferson

J. Raiford J. P.

William Paulett, Sheriff Jefferson County [115]
Jno. Paulett, D. Sheriff

P. Richardson

Bird Tarver
R. D. Gray
M. Schley
Duglass Hancock
Joseph Hampton
James Neely

Hor. Mallbury
M. Shelman
Patrick Conelly
Thacker Vivion, Sen.
Thacker Vivion, Jn^{r}
John Green, 2nd Lt.
Garland Hardwick, S. C.
Benjamin Mayo, J. P.
Hor. Maibury
Walter Robinson, J. P.

M. O. A. Johnson, Mayor
Jesse Loflen
Alex^{r} Carswell   M. Bostick

27 Feby 1801
Absalom Pryor
23rd March 1801
R. D. Gray
23 March 1801
Charles C. Finkens
7 April 1801
Joseph Tomne
1 May 1801
Wm Hammok
1 May 1801
Elijah Christiefert
16 May 1801
Elias Hodges

Seth Gates
Jno. W. Berrier
T. Brown
James Danby
Jno. Worth
M. Sterrett

We do hereby nominate Mr. George Stapleton a Justice of the Peace in Captain Terrys [116] district in the room Robert Patterson who refuses to act. June 27th 1799. M. Shelman, D. Hancock, R. Gray

We do Solemnly or affirm that we will bear true faith and allegiance to the State of Georgia and to the utmost of my power and abilities observe, conform to, support, & defend the Constitution thereof, without any reservation or equivocation whatsoever; and the Constitution of the United States, so help me God. G. W. Hardwick 27th July 1803

James Bassnon, Ensign
A. Hammond
Ja^{s} Bohanon 15th July 1803

Isaac Robinson
M. Shelman
Clerk of the S. Court J.

Georgia }
Jefferson County }
At an Inferior Court held in and for County aforesaid [117]
on the 11th day of July 1799. Present, their Honors Duglass Hancock, Thacker Vivion, M. Shelman, John Clements

Philip Clayton }
vs } Case
John Lewis }

I do hereby confess a Judgment for the Sum of Two hundred & fifty dollars with Interest from the first day of Octr one thousand Seven hundred & 98 & Cost with Stay of execution until the first day of November next. H. G. Caldwell, atty for John Lewis

John Hammond, for the use }
of Seaborn Jones }
vs } Case
Abner Hammond }

I confess Judgment for the Sum of Seventy Six dollars eighty one & ¼ Cents, with Cost, with Stay of Levy three months from this day. 11 July 1799. H. G. Caldwell. for A. Hammond Judgment entered. Satisfaction Entered up.

Cornelius Dysart, for the use }
of H. Russell }
vs } Case
John Cobbs }

I do confess Judgment for the Sum of four hundred & Sixty Six dollars and twenty five Cents, with Stay of Levy upon payment of Cost, till first December next. 11 July 1799. John Cobbs. Judgment entered.

Asa Avery } [119]
vs } Debt
G. W. Chisolm }

I do hereby appear and confess a Judgment to Asa Avery for the Sum of Seventy one dollars & seventy three Cents, and Costs of Suit, with a Stay of Levy three months from this date. July 11, 1799. Peter J. Carnes, Att^y for Defend^t

John L. Dixon, for the use }
of John Hamil }
vs } Case
Jesse Newton }

Jurors Sworn

1. John Darby	7. John McMahan
2. James McMullan	8. Wm Spivy
3. Wm Baker	9. James Hall
4. John Ford	10. Redden Hall
5. N. Whitaker	11. Thomp^s Lawson
6. Robt Stone	12. Wm Liggett

We find for the Plaintiff forty nine dollars, twelve and an half cents, with Cost of Suit. N. Whitaker, foreman. Judgment ent[d]

Daniel Hart } [120]
vs } Case
De Leiben & Posner }

Same Jury as before. We find for the Plaintiff three hundred and eighty one dollars and Seventy five cents with Cost of Suit. N. Whitaker, foreman. Judgment entered.

Edward Ford }
vs } Debt
Thomas Shields }

Same Jury as before. We find for the Plaintiff three hundred and Twenty Seven dollars and twenty five cents with Costs of Suit. 11 July 1799. N. Whitaker, foreman. Judgment entered.

John Lewis } [121]
vs } Case
Alex. Love }

Same Jury as before. We find for the Plaintiff Sixty nine dollars and ninety six cents, with Cost of Suit. N. Whitaker, foreman

David Robinson }
vs } Case
Blas[s] Harvey, Sen[r] }

By consent, it is order[d] that Richard Gray, esq[r], or Dan[l] Sturges, esq[r], be and he is hereby required to allerd and resurvey a Tract of land sold by the defendant to the Plaintiff Adjoining the Queensboro line & Stubbs land and return affair copy thereof to this Court and that each party have a due notice of this order.

Joseph G. Posner }
vs } Case
John Cobbs }

I do hereby confess a Judgment for the Sum of eighty five dollars & Twenty five cents & Cost. 11 July 1799. John Cobbs

Philip Clayton } [122]
vs } Case
John Cobbs }

It is mually agreed between the parties, that all matters in despute between them be referred to the determination and arbitration of James Meriwether, Peter J. Carnes, & Thomas Flournay, esquires, whose award shall be final, without the power of appealing, provided that the same be entered under the hands & Seals of the said arbitrators at or before the next term of this Court, so as to be made the Judgment, and that either of the parties may appoint a time for the arbitrators to meet, provided they give the opposing party twenty days notice of the time and place of meeting, which shall be in the Town of Louisville.

John Stokes } [123]
vs }
Jesse Miles & Ash Wood }

Same Jury as before. We find for the Plaintiff forty two dollars twelve and an half cents, with Cost of Suit. N. Whitaker, foreman.

M. Shelman, J. I. C^{t}, John Clements, Duglass Hancock

Friday morning, July 12th 1799. Court met Agreeably to Adjournment. Present, their honors [124]
Thacker Vivion, M. Shelman, Duglass Hancock

The Commiss^{rs} of Burke }
Academy }
vs } fi fa
John Cobbs, Jno L. Dixon & }
Alexander Love }

On Motion of the Plaintiffs Councill it is ordered that the Sheriff do make return of the execution in the above Case or show cause at 1 o'clock tomorrow morning why an attachment should not issue against him for contempt.

Ananias Cooper } [125]
vs } Case
Alexander Love }

John Cobbs came into Court and acknowledges himself special bail in the above case to pay the eventual condemnation money or to deliver the body of the defendant in discharge thereof. A. Love, Jn. Cobbs. Test. Jas. Bozeman.

John Berrier }
vs } Special Case
Thomas Johnson }

The Plaintiff in the above case being three times called, and not answering, the Court adjudged the Plaintiff nonsuited.

Richard Dennis }
vs } case
Posner & Benedix }

Same Jury as before. We find for the Plaintiff fifteen hundred & fifty two dollars & Twenty three cents, with Interest & Cost of Suit.

John McQueen for the use } [126]
of H. Hampton }
vs } Caveat
John Cobbs }

a Juror withdraws and a Nonsuit.

John Rushen }
vs } Case
Alex. Love }

I do hereby confess Judgment for the Sum of one hundred and seventy eight dollars and fourteen cents & Cost. Stay of Levy until the 15th Decr next. 12 July 1799. H. Caldwell, for Defendant

John L. Heffer for the use }
of Jno Rushen }
vs } Case
Alexander Love }

I do hereby confess Judgment for the sum of Thirty five dollars & fifty two & ½ cts & Cost with Stay of levy until the 15th Decr next. H. G. Caldwell for defendant. 12 July 1799.

Posner & Benedix } [127]
vs }
Jesse Paulett & }
David Paulett }

Settled at the Plaintiffs Cost.

Posner & Benedix }
vs } Case
David Terry }

I do hereby confess Judgment for the Sum of forty Six dollars forty eight & ¾ Cents & Cost & with three months Stay of Levy. 12th July 1799. David Terry

Philip Clayton }
vs } Case
Zachr Gray }

Jurors Sworn

1. Stephen Morgan	5. Saml Mayo	9. John Blair
2. Joab Horn	6. Benj. Dasse	10. Jas. Neely
3. Wm Fountain	7. Solo. Willy	11. Wm Peel
4. Ruben Ross	8. Wm McBride	12. J. M. Sterret

We find for the Plaintiff one hundred & thirty six dollars Sixty two & ½ Cents with interest & Cost. Jos. M. Sterrett

Hugh Alexander } [128]
vs } application for letters dismissory
Martha Yeaton }
Adimistratrix of }
Thomas Alexander, decd }

The defendant came into open Court and acknowledged that Hugh Alexander, Executor of the estate of Thomas Alexander, deceased, should be finally discharged, released, and forever acquitted of all and Singular the Charges, demands, or accounts that have been or may be brought against him as Executor of the estate of the aforesaid Thomas Alexander, deceased. 12 July 1799. Martha Yeaton

Thomas Whitehead }
vs }
Absalom Wells } Bail discharged

Court Adjourned till tomorrow morning 9 o'Clock. Test. Jas. Bozeman, Clk. M. Shelman [129]
Duglass Hancock, Thack Vivion

Saturday, July 13th 1799. Court met agreeably to adjournment. Present, their honors M. Shelman, Tha. Vivion, D. Hancock

John & M. Shelman }
vs } case
Tandy C. Key } Settled at defendants Cost.

M. Shelman }
vs } Case
Tandy C. Key } Settled at defendants Cost.

Nathan Powell } [130]
vs } Case
John Golding }

Jurors Sworn

1. John Darby	7. John McMahan
2. W. Dawkins	8. Wm Spiers
3. Jos. Chears	9. Jas. Hall
4. N. Whitaker	10. Redden Hall
5. Robt Stone	11. Thompson Lawson
6. Wm Evans	12. Wm Leggitt

We find for the Plaintiff fifty nine dollars fifty seven & an half cents, with Interest & Cost of Suit. N. Whitaker, foreman

Saml McKee }
vs } Case
Bless. Harvey, Sen. }

1. Stephen Morgan	7. W. McBride
2. Joab Horn	8. John Blair
3. W. Fountain	9. Jas. Neely
4. Rueb. Ross	10. Z. Gray
5. Saml Mayo	11. Thos. Peebles
6. Sollomon Willy	12. Nathl Williams

We find no cause of action. John Blair, foreman

Isaac Rawls } [131]
vs } Attachment
Mathias Dalton }

1. John Darby	7. John McMahan
2. Wm Dawkins	8. Wm Spiers
3. Joseph Chears	9. Jas. Hall
4. N. Whitaker	10. Redden Hall
5. Robt Stone	11. Thomp. Lawson
6. Wm Evans	12. Wm Leggitt

We find for the Plaintiff Eleven dollars with Cost of Suit. N. Whitaker, foreman

David B. Butler }
vs } Case
John Cobbs }

The defendant having failed to appear and put in his Answer, it is considered that Judgment pass against him by default. J. Hamill, O. V. Aty.

Isaac Rawls } [132]
vs } Attachment
Mathias Dalton }

The defendant in this case came within the time allowed by law, claimed an appeal and having complied with the terms of the act, It was granted and Blass. Harvey, Sen[r] became his Security for the prosecution thereof in Terms of the law. Blass. X Harvey, his mark. M. X Dalton, his mark

Thomas Hart }
vs } Attachment
James Andrews }

The defendant being three times duly called , did not answer & thereupon Judgment by def[t] was ent[d] up against him.

James Wallace }
vs } Assumit
Thomas Shields }

The defendant, Thomas Shields, doth confess a Judgment to the Plaintiff, James Wallace, for the amount of Seventeen hundred and fifty dollars, with interest from the time note became due, with a Stay of execution till the first day of march next, ensuing acknowledged in open Court. Thomas Shields. July 13th 1799

Commiss[rs] of Burke }
Academy }
vs }
W[m] Paulett, Sheriff }

The Sheriff having paid the amount of Principal, interest & Cost in this Case into Court,. It is thereupon ordered that the rule of Yesterday to shew cause be discharged.

Court adjourned till the. M. Shelman, Duglass Hancock, Thac[k] Vivion

Richard Dennis }
vs }
Posner & Benedix } [134]

The defendant in this case came within the time allowed by law, claims an appeal, and having complied with the terms of the act, it was granted & John Scott became his security for the prosecution in terms of the law. Jas. G. Posner. Jno Scott

Daniel Hart }
vs } Case
De Leiben & Posner }

The defendant in this case came within the time allowed by law, claims an appeal, and having complied with the terms of the act, it was granted & John Scott became his security for the prosecution in terms of the law. Jas. G. Posner. Jno Scott

Philip Clayton } [135]
vs }
Zachariah Gray }

The defendant in this case came within the time allowed by law, claims an appeal, and having complied with the terms of the act, it was granted and Nathan Powell became his security for the prosecution in terms of the law. Zach Gray. N. Powell

Nathan Powell }
vs }
John Golden }

In this case, the defendant and Morris Gilbert came to the clerks office and bound themselves Jointly and Severally to the Plaintiff for the amount of the Verdict, for Stay of execution Sixty days. July 18th 1799. John Golden. Morris Gilbert.

Friday, the 19th July 1799. The Inferior Court met agreeably to adjournment. Present, their honors Thacker Vivion, Michael Shelman, Duglass Hancock

Ordered, That Abraham Coursey be and he is hereby appointed Constable for Captain Terrys district.

Ordered, That William Ford be and is hereby appointed a Constable for Captain Keys district.

On an application of James Green, for a Guardian for his person & property. [137]
Ordered, That Joseph Chears be and is hereby appointed Guardian of the person & property of

the said James Green. And the said Joseph Chears do give bond & security in the sum of four hundred dollars for the faithful performance thereof.

On the application of Joseph White, Sally Jenkins, & Epsey Wallace, praying that Epsey Wallace (who was at July Term last, bound out to the said Joseph White by Indenture) Should be discharged from her said Indenture, and the said Joseph White also discharged from his bond in that behalf, and that the said Epsey Wallace be placed under the protection of her Sister Sally

Jenkins. [138]
It is ordered that the said Epsey Wallace be discharged from her Indenture and the said Joseph White also discharged from his obligation as to the support of her, the said Epsey Wallace, and that the said Sally Jinkins do agreeably to her own will and consent, as now expressed to the Court, take charge of and support the said Epsey Wallace, her sister.

Court adjourned till tomorrow morning ten o'Clock. Attest. Jas. Bozeman, Clk

Saturday, July 20th 1799. The Court met agreeably to adjournment. Present, their [139]
honors M. Shelman, D. Hancock, Th. Vivion, Judges of the said Ct

On the application of David Thomas praying a license to retail Spirituous liquours in less quantities that one quart. It is ordered, That the clerk do issue license accordingly, upon taking bond & Security as the law directs.

On the application of Thomas Cox praying a license to retail Spirituous liquors in less Quantities that one quart. It is or, that the Clerk do issue license accordingly, upon taking bond and Security as the law directs.

On the application of Daniel Limle praying a license to retail Spirituous liquors in less [140]
quantities that one quart. It is ordered, That the clerk do issue license accordingly, upon taking bond & Security as the law directs.

On the application of Walter Robinson praying a license to retail Spirituous liquors in less quantities that one quart. It is ordered, That the clerk do issue license accordingly, upon taking bond & Security as the law directs.

A list of Jurors drawn to Serve at the next term, that of January term 1800. [141]

1. Jno Green	22. Herman Mayo
2. Saml McBride	23. Josias Fountain
3. Wm Whigham	24. Jno Parsons
4. Reuben Waldon	25. Luke Slaughter
5. Wm Manson	26. Robt Foil
6. Jno Burton	27. Danl McNeil

7. Herman Ross
8. Eph. Kennidy
9. Jno Wilson
10. Wm Parsons
11. Danl Thomas
12. Hugh Gilmore
13. Wm Herren
14. Jno Hamack
15. Saml McCandles
16. Jno Womack
17. Saml Sandford
18. Robt Greevy
19. Fred. Clem
20. John Reese
21. Robt Morril
28. N. Sample
29. Tho. Peebles
30. Ja^{s} Martin
31. Tho. Girvin
32. Esom. Franklin
33. Step. Dirensaux
34.Ginnings Cottle
35. John Rice
36. John Morris
37. Saml Little
38. Jno Padget
39. Abram Baily
40. John Foil
41. Richd Corbet
42. Thomas Gay
43. Lem Page
44. Robt Little
45. Wm Ford
46. Wm Harris
47. Abel Sutton
48. Jesse Glover

On the application of Jane Donaldson, administratrix of the estate of Geo. Donaldson, [142]
deceased, for an order of Sale of a Tract of land containing two hundred and fifty acres in Jefferson County, formerly Queensboro Township, on the waters of Chavers' Creek, granted to the said George Donaldson, dec^{d}, for the benefit of the heirs & Creditors, and it appearing to the Court that notice of Such application has been published in one of the public Gazettes of this State the time required by law, no persons appearing to gainsay the same, It is ordered that the said administratrix be authorized to make sale of the said land, upon publicly notifying the same in terms of the law.

On the application of Chesley Bostwick, administrator of the Estate & Effects of Charles [143]
Watson, deceased, for an order of Sale of part of the real estate of the said Charles Watson, deceased, to wit. Eight hundred Acres in Jefferson County, when Survey^{d} in the Parish of St. George, granted to said Watson and bounded by cavenoh and Vacant land, for the benefit of the Heirs & Creditors; and it appearing to the Court that notice of such application had been published nine months in one of the public Gazettes, It is therefore ordered that a Sale thereof be granted upon the administrators publishing a further notice of the Sale in terms of the law.

Ordered, That William Gold Carnes be allowed the Sum of fifteen dollars and fifty cents [144]
agreeably to his account filed in the office of this Court & that the Clerk do pay the same.

Ordered, That one fourth part of the amt. of the General tax be levied for County uses and that the Collector do give bond for the Collection of the same agreeably to law.

Ordered that the Clerk do issue an execution against Alexander Carswell for five dollars for not attending at July Term 1798 as a Juror drawn to serve at that Term.

Ordered, That Walter Robinson be and he is hereby appointed a Commissioner of the Road [145] leading from Louisville, to intersect a new road opened from Grays Mill to Philip Claytons, in addition to the former commissioners.

Ordered, That Thacker Vivion, esq[r], be and he is hereby authorised to contract with some person to furnish plank for covering the bridge across Williamsons swamp, Known and called Vivions Bridge, and that he do draw on the Clerk for the payment of the same out of any monies that may come into his hands.

Court adjourned till court in course. Jas. Bozeman, Clk

Edward Ford } [146]
vs } Case
Thomas Shields }

In the above case, came Peregrine F. Bayard & Thomas Shields, Jun[r] and entered Security for the payment of the Judgm[t] obtained in the Inferior Court July Term 1799 on the first day of January next. Thos. Shields, Pereg. F. Bayard, Thomas Shields, J[r]

Ordered, That Thomas Whitehead, Andrew Hampton, and John Whigham be and they are [147] hereby Appointed Commissioners to keep in good repair the road leading from Louisville to Whiteheads, and from thence to the Chickasaw bridge on brier Creek.

Inferior Court, Jefferson County, Sept[r] 9 1799 [148]

John Bostick & }
John Wallace }
vs } Casa issued from the Justices Court
Dan[l] McDowell }

On the Petition of Daniel McDowell, setting forth that he is confined in Jail by virtue of a writ of Capeas – ad. Satisfaciendum issued out of the Justices Court of the Town of Louisville at the Suits of John Bostick and John Wallace, and that he is unable to support himself during such his confinement and praying to be admitted to the benefit of the Act of the General Assembly in such cases made and provided. It is ordered that notification be twice published in one of the Gazettes, that all persons concerned do attend at the Clerks office on Saturday the twenty first Ins[t] to show cause, if any they have, why the petitioner should not be discharged

Agreeably to the prayer of the petition and that a copy of this order be served on the Plaintiffs or their atty. [149]

Ordered that the tax collector of Jefferson County for the year 1798 be authorised to collect the Taxes due to the County aforesaid by John Bowman for Sixteen hundred Acres of land in said County for the years 1796, 1797, & 1798. September 21st 1799

A Schedule of the estate both real and personal of Daniel McDowell, an insolvent, to wit. A list of debts owing the said D. McDowell by Sundry persons.

Mathew Golding	$2.00	
Nathan Daniel	5.00	
William Lawson	14.62½	
William	4.00	
John Wallace	5.85	
Nancy Breedlove	15.6½	$46.54

I Daniel McDowell do Solemnly Swear, in the presence of Almighty God, that
I am not possessed of any real or personal Estate, debts, credits, or effects whatsoever, [150]
my wearing apparel, working tools excepted, other than are contained in the Schedule now delivered and that I have not directly or indirectly, since my imprisonment or before, sold, leased, assigned, or otherwise disposed of, or made over, in trust for myself or otherwise, any part of my lands, estate, Goods, Stock, money, or debts, or other real or personal estate whereby to have or expect any benefit or profit to myself or my heirs, so help me God. September 21, 1799

Ordered, That the said Daniel McDowell be set at liberty on paying all fees due since his imprisonment to the Goaler, also all that he may earn hereafter during his confinement until said fees are paid.

Ordered, That Duett Dees, William Cauthorn, and Simon Smith be and they are hereby [151]
appointed Commissrs to lay off and open a road leading from where the Savannah Road intersects the County line, between Montgomery County and Jefferson, by Powells Mill, thence the nearest and best way to Sandersville, as far as the County line. September 21st 1799

Ordered, that Joseph Hampton, esqr, Jesse Brown, and James Young be appointed Commissrs to keep in good repair that part of the old Quaker road leading Genl Trigg's mill thro the County of Jefferson. September 21 1799.

Ordered, That Bird Tarver be and he is hereby nominated a Justice of the Peace for Captain Tarvers district in the room of William Clements, who declind accepting his Commission. Septr 21 1799

M. Shelman, Duglass Hancock, R. D. Gray

Ordered, That John Scott be and he is hereby nominated a Justice of the Peace for Captain Johnsons district, in the room of James Merewether, who declined accepting his Commission. October 8th 1799. M. Shelman, R. D. Gray, John Clements [152]

At an Inferior Court began and held at Louisville, Jefferson County, on the third Monday in January 1800, being the 20th day of the same month. Present Duglass Hancock, Thacker Vivion, Zach^{r} Lamar, Judges of the said Court [153]

John Neely }
vs } Case
John Lewis }

Jurors sworn

1. John Cottle	7. Wm Ford
2. Robt Foil	8. Hugh Gilmore
3. Wm Manson	9. John Green
4. Lem^{l} Page	10. Richd Corbitt
5. Jno Hammack	11. Jno Padget
6. Tho. Girvin	12. Danl McNeil

We find for the Commissioners two hundred and Eighteen dollars eighty three cents, with Cost of Suit. Wm Ford, foreman

Joel & William Walker } [154]
vs } Case
John & William Clements } Dismissed

Court adjourned till tomorrow 9 o'Clock. Test. Jas. Bozeman, Clk.

Tuesday, the 21st Jany 1800 the Court agreeably to adjournment. Present, the Honorable Duglass Hancock, Richd Gray, Z. Lamar, Judges

Rachel Taylor, Jesse Britt, & }
Owen Fort }
vs }
Jas. Dees }

1. John Cottle	7. Wm Ford
2. Robert Foil	8. H. Gilmore
3. Wm Manson	9. Tho. Peebles
4. Lem^{l} Page	10. Richd Corbitt
5. Nathl Sample	11. Jno Padget
6. Tho. Girvin	12. Danl McNeil

We find for the Plaintiff forty four dollars & thirty nine Cents, with Cost of Suit. Wm Ford, Foreman

Posner & Benedix } [155]
vs }
Vinson Rowell }

Same Jury as before.

We find for the Plaintiffs three and seventy dollars & fifty cents, with Interest from the 1 Jany 1798 & Cost. William Ford, Foreman

Benjamin Acock }
vs }
A. Pierce & C. Rhodes }

The parties submit their difference in this Suit to the arbitrument and final award of Michael Shelman, Burrel Jourdon, John Lawrence, and Solomon Wood, with a power on the Referees to chose an umpire. The Arbitrators to me meet at Robert Fullwoods plantation and to act on their own Adjournment until they make up their award. Provided a return of said award be made to the next term of the Inferior Court, then and there to be made a Judgement of the said Court.

John & Michael Shelman } [156]
vs } Case
William McGehee }

By consent of parties, it is ordered that all matters in dispute in the above Case be submitted to the final Arbitratment and award of Thomas Collier, James Merewether, & Walter Robinson, Esquires, whose award shall be returned on or before the last day of the next term and be then and there made the final Judgment of the Court.

Notice being given that Application will be made for an order to sell the real Estate of Robert Hamilton, deceased, for the benefit of the Heirs and Creditors of the said Hamilton. Thomas R. E. Hamilton, by Peter Harris his Attorney, shews cause against an order of Court being granted to sell the Estate aforesaid.

1st because the application is not of the rightful and legal administrator of the decd. [157]
2nd That it is not necessary for the benefit of the Heirs and Creditors of the decd that the real estate of the aforesaid Robert Hamilton should be sold and disposed of as set forth in the Notice above mentioned.

Whereupon, it is ordered that the parties concerned attend at the next Inferior Court for Jefferson County when the said Court will do as Justice shall appertain.

Posner & Benedix }
vs }
Jn° Cobbs }

Same Jury as before.

We find for the Plaintiffs the Sum of Seven hundred and ninety four dollars thirty seven and an half Cents and by the consent of the Plaintiff all Just receipts for payment made to or Cotton received by the Plaintiffs are to be deducted of the same are produced within Sixty days from this day. Wm Ford, foreman

Court adjourned till tomorrow morning 9 o'clock. Rest. Jas. Bozeman, Clk. [158]

Wednesday, the 22nd January 1800. Court met agreeably to adjournment. Present Duglass Hancock, Richd Gray, Z. Lamar, Judges of the said Court.

Thomas Jones }
vs } Case
James Jackson }

Order^d^ that the Clerk of the Court do certify and send up to the next Superior Court all the proceedings in the above Case.

Philip Clayton } [159]
vs }
Jn° Cobbs }

I do hereby confess Judgment for the sum of Eight hundred and thirty dollars on this Proviso, that all legal sets off offered within Sixty days are to be discounted out of said Judgment with a Stay of levy nine months. 23rd January 1800. Jn° Cobbs

Baldwin Flaker }
vs }
John Paulett & }
James Harvey }

Jurors Sworn

1. Jn° Cottle	7. Wm Ford
2. Robert Foil	8. Hugh Gilmore
3. Lem^l^ Page	9. Thomas Peebles
4. Reuben Walden	10. Richard Corbit
5. Thomas Girvin	11. Jn° Hamack
6. Wm Manson	12. Danl McNeil

We find for the Plaintiff in case Eighty eight dollars and Twenty cents, with Cost of Suit. 23 Jany 1800. Wm Ford, Foreman

David B. Butler } [160]
vs }
John Cobbs }

I confess a Judgment to the Plaintiff for the Sum of Two hundred and thirty five dollars & fourteen Cents & Cost, with Stay of levy Sixty days. Jno Cobbs

William Smith }
vs }
Isaac Auger }

Same Jury as before.

We find for the Plaintiff fifty Eight dollars with Cost of Suit. William Ford, Foreman

Mathias Dalton }
vs }
Isaac Rawls }

Dismissed at the Plaintiffs Cost.

William Butler } [161]
vs }
John Cobbs }

I do hereby confess Judgment for the sum of Twenty two dollars & eighty five cents, with Interest from the thirty first day of March one thousand seven hundred ninety four, with Stay of levy or execution Sixty days. 22 day Jany 1800. Jno Cobbs

James Hutchenson }
vs }
John Cobbs }

I do hereby confess Judgment for the sum of two hundred and fifty seven dollars fifteen Cents, with Interest from the eleventh day of August one thousand seven hundred ninety five, with Stay of levy or execution Sixty days. 22nd Jany 1800. Jno Cobbs

William Collins } [162]
vs }

Rob[t] Fullwood & }
Nath[l] Knotts }

Same Jury.

We find for the Plaintiff one hundred and Twenty dollars, with interest & Cost of Suit. William Ford, foreman

William Collins }
vs }
Robert Fullwood & }
Tho[s] H. Kenan }

Same Jury.

We find for the Plaintiff three hundred & nineteen dollars & 68 Cents, with interest & Cost of Suit. W[m] Ford, foreman

Nathaniel Barton }
assignee of Jn[o] Hamack }
vs } Case
Jesse Newton & }
E. Jencks }

Same Jury as before.

We the Jury find for the Plaintiff one hundred & Twenty dollars, with lawful interest & Cost of Suit. W[m] Ford, Foreman

Posner & Benedix } [163]
vs }
Jn[o] Cobbs }

The defendant in this case came within the time allowed by law, claimed an appeal, and having complied with the terms of the law, it was granted, and Eldridge Hargrove became his Security in terms of the law. Jn[o] Cobbs. E. Hargrove.

Thomas Carr }
vs } Covenant
Robert Jackson & }
John Fore }

Same Jury as before.

We find for the Plaintiff four hundred dollars with Cost of Suit. Wm Ford, foreman

Annanias Cooper } [164]
vs } Case
Alexander Love }

Same Jury as before.

We find for the Plaintiff three hundred and forty five dollars, with Cost of Suit. Wm Ford, foreman

Court adjourned till tomorrow morning 10 o'clock. Test. Jas. Bozeman, Clk

John Neely } [165]
vs }
John Lewis }

In this case, the defendant came within the time allowed by law, claimed an appeal, and having complied with the terms of the Act, it was granted, and Vinson Rowell became his Security for the prosecution thereof in terms of the law. John Lewis. Vinson Rowell.

Posner & Benedix }
vs }
Vinson Rowell }

In this case, the defendant came within the time allowed by law, claimed an Appeal, and having complied with the terms of the Act, it was granted, and John Lewis became his Security for the prosecution thereof in terms of the law. Vinson Rowell. John Lewis.

Thursday, the 23rd day of January 1800. Court met agreeably to adjournment. Present [166]
their Michael Shelman, Thacker Vivion, Zachr Lamar, Judges of said Court.

William Collins }
vs }
Robt Fullwood & }
Thos H. Kenan }

In this case, the defendant came within the time allowed by law, claimed an Appeal, and having complied with the terms of the Act, it was granted, and Abraham Pierce became his Security for the prosecution thereof in terms of the law. R. Fullwood. Abraham Pierce.

Carpenter & Harvey }
vs }
Posner & Benedix } [167]

Bail discharged & Term given.

Rachel Taylor }
Jesse Brett & }
Owen Fort }
vs }
Jas. Dais }

In this case, the defendant came within the time Allowed by law, claimed an Appeal, and having complied with the terms of the Act, it was granted, and Robert Fullwood became his Security for the prosecution thereof in terms of the law. James Dees. R. Fullwood.

Court Adjourned till the fourteenth day of february next to do the County business. Attest. Jas. Bozeman, Clk

William Collins } [168]
vs }
Robert Fullwood }
& Nath[l] Knotts }

In this case, the defendant came within the time Allowed by law, claimed an appeal, and having complied with the terms of the Act, it was granted, and Thacker Vivion became his Security for the prosecution thereof in terms of the law. R. Fullwood. Thacker Vivion.

Friday, the 14th February 1800. The Court met agreeably to adjournment and proceeded to the business of the Court of Ordinary, and adjourned till tomorrow 9 o'clock. Test. Jas Bozeman, Clk

Saturday, the 15th February 1800. The Court met agreeably to adjournment. Present, their honors Michael Shelman, Duglass Hancock, Richard Gray, Judges of the said Court. [169]

Horatio Marbury and John Scott, esquires, having sent in to this Court their resignations as Justices of the Peace for the distict of Louisville.

Ordered, That John Berrier and Thomas Collier be and they are hereby nominated Justices of the Peace for the district of Louisville, in the room of Horatio Marbury & John Scott, who resigned.

Bird Tarver having sent to this Court his resignation as a Justice of the Peace for Captain Tarvers district. Ordered, That Ashly Wood be and he is hereby nominated a Justice of the Peace for Captain Tarvers district.

Ordered, That Robert Fullwood, esquire, receiver of the returns of taxable property, be [170] allowed two and one half per Cent on the amount of the County tax for the year 1799.

On the application of Elizabeth Palmer, Administratrix of all and Singular the goods and Chattels which were of Edward Palmer, dec^d, for the Sale of a House and Lot Situate in the town of Louisville, bounded Southeastward by Walnut Street, Eastwardly by lot N° 194, and on all other sides by alleys, known in the plan of the said Town by N° 173, for the benefit of the heirs and Creditors, it being part of the real Estate of the said Edward Palmer, dec^d, and it appearing Satisfactory to the Court that a notice of this application had been duly published for the term of nine Months and no person appearing to gainsay the same. It is therefore ordered that a Sale do accordingly take place in terms of the law in such cases made & provided.

Ordered, That the Clerk of the Superior Court, as also the Clerk of this Court, do lay before [171] this Court at their next meeting a Statement of all County monies that may be in their hands respectively, that may have arisen from the sale of estrays, fines, or forfeitures.

Court adjourned till friday, the 21 Inst. Jas. Bozeman, Clk. R. D. Gray, J. P., M. Shelman, Duglass Hancock

Friday, the 21st February 1800. The Court met agreeably to adjournment & adjourned till thursday, the 27th Instant. Test. Jas. Bozeman, Clk

Thursday, the 27th February 1800. The Court met agreeably to adjournment. Present, [172] their honors Duglass Hancock, Michael Shelman, Richard Gray, Thacker Vivion, Zachariah Lamar.

Ordered that one fourth part of the amount of the General tax be levied s a County tax for the year 1800 and that the Collector do give bond for the Collection thereof agreeably to law.

On the application of Louis Voicle praying a license to keep a house of entertainment. It is ordered that the Clerk do issue to the said Voicle a license on his giving bond with Sufficient Security agreeably to law, to be approved by anyone of the Court.

On the application of Jonathan Hilton praying a license to keep a house of entertainment. [173] It is ordered that the Clerk do issue to the said Hilton a license on his giving bond with Sufficient Security agreeably to law, to be approved by anyone of the Court.

Ordered, That the Clerk do pay to Jas. Paulett, Sheriff, Six dollars and 12½ Cents out of the County tax as pr account rendered.

Ordered, That Hezekiah Gates be and he is hereby appointed Commissioner of the road leading from Louisville to Georgetown in the room of Charles Harvey, resigned.

Ordered that the Commissioners for building a Court house and Jail be and they are hereby authorised to draw on the Clerk of this Court for three hundred dollars to be paid out of any monies that now is or thereafter may come into his hands as County Tax for the year 1799, to be by them applied for the purpose of erecting a court house. And that the Clerk of this Court be authorised to receipt to the Clerk of the Superior Court for any monies that now is or hereafter may come into his hands by fines, forfeiting, or the Sale of estrays.

Ordered, That the Clerk of this Court to pay to Joseph Chears thirty dollars out of any monies that may come into his hands on account of Court house rent.

Ordered, That Joseph Chears be and is hereby appointed Commissioner of the road leading [175]
from Louisville to Savannah, in room of William A. Brackett, deceased.

Ordered, That the Clerk do issue a license for keeping a house of entertainment to William Herren, on his giving bond and Security in terms of the act, gratuitously on account of his indigence and infirm Situation.

Court adjourned till court in course. M. Shelman, Z. Lamar, R. D. Gray

13th April 1800.

Ordered that Horatio Marbury & Walter Robinson be and they are hereby appointed Justices of the Peace for Louisville district, in lieu of Jno Barrien & Thomas Collier, who were nominated for said district on the 15th February 1800 & which his Excellency the Governor cannot Commission as appears by the official information of his Excellency to Duglas Hancock, Esqr. R. D. Gray, Z. Lamar, Duglass Hancock

Docket of Executions returnable to Decr term 1797. [176]

1. Jno Shelman }
vs } $5.00 3 issued 16 Nov 1797
Jno Anderson }

2. Levin Collins }
vs } $93 16 Nov 1797
Zach. Gray }

3. Bailey Harrell }
vs } $32 16 Nov 1797
Harvey & Key }

4. Jeremiah Oats }
vs } $32 16 Nov 1797
Jesse Paulett }

5. Ananias Cooper }
vs } $69 27 Nov 1797
William Ross }

6. Ben. Forsyth }
vs } $143.74 27 Nov 1797
Heirs of Christian }

Index

Wm., 42

Wm., Sr., 11

www.ingramcontent.com/pod-product-compliance
Lightning Source LLC
Chambersburg PA
CBHW070256290326
41930CB00041B/2607
* 9 7 8 0 8 0 6 3 5 7 6 7 6 *